GEMS
from Joan

WE WILL REMEMBER

Scripture quotations used in this book are taken from the following versions:

The Holy Bible, King James Version. The Living Bible, copyright © 1971. Used by permission of Tyndale House Publishers, Inc. P.O. Box 80, Wheaton, Illinois 60189. New American Standard Bible®, copyright © 1960, 1962, 1963, 1968, 1971, 1972, 1973, 1975, 1977, 1995 by The Lockman Foundation. Used by permission. The Holy Bible, New International Version, copyright © 1973, 1978, 1984, International Bible Society. Used by permission of Zondervan Bible Publishers. Holy Bible, New Living Translation, copyright © 1996, 2004. Used by permission of Tyndale House Publishers, Inc, Wheaton, Illinois 60189. All rights reserved. The Holy Bible, Today's New International Version, copyright © 2001 by International Bible Society. All rights reserved. New Testament in Modern English translated by J. B. Phillips, copyright © 1958, 1959, 1960, 1972 by J. B. Phillips.

Compiled and edited by Andrea Horner, Ph.D., and Mary Horner Collins
Cover design and interior design by Melanie Johnson.

Printed in the United States of America

2011— First printing

WE WILL REMEMBER

*J*oan Horner (1925-2010) changed countless lives around the world with her messages of hope and encouragement, and her passion for keeping it personal. She lived out her faith and her example continues to inspire us all.

This is a book of remembrance for our Premier Designs family—a compendium of Joan's written and spoken messages over the years. It's designed to be a volume you can pick up anytime you're in need of encouragement or wisdom, whether you have five minutes or fifteen. We've organized the book into seven sections to make it easier to locate a message by topic. It's like having Joan as your mentor—right at your fingertips. Plus, this collection is a valuable tool for you as you mentor others.

The best way we can show we remember Joan is to embrace the ideas she shared with us, and commit ourselves anew to enriching every life we are able to touch—serving with love and integrity, without expecting anything in return.

CONTENTS

A WORD FROM ANDY HORNER

*J*oan was a gift from heaven to me. She was so very, very special. Her love for our Lord Jesus Christ and her love for people helped make Premier Designs the unique company—and family—it is today. We will remember Joan, her sweet smile, her quiet nature, and the many ways she enriched all of our lives. We'll remember her mission "to keep it personal," and how she wanted to make sure every person knew they were "somebody special," made in the image of our loving and personal God.

This volume of remembrance contains enduring words of wisdom—gems, compiled with diligence and loving care by our daughters Andrea and Mary, from various written and spoken messages Joan shared over the years with our Premier family and others. So much of what she shared was rooted in the Bible, an expression of her deep faith. She had a message of truth and hope to share that would provide insights no matter what your faith. Her goal was always to challenge and inspire, encouraging us to live beyond ourselves and to "count it all joy" no matter what the circumstances.

We've also included some of the stories Joan loved to tell to illustrate her points. Some of those are pretty funny. She loved to laugh!

Recently, while going through one of Joan's keepsake boxes, my daughters found a letter that I wrote to Joan back in 1964. That letter expressed what I felt then, and it expresses how I feel now.

December 22, 1964

My Dear Joan:

It is so difficult for me at this time of year to find a gift which fully expresses my love and appreciation of you. Many times I have told you how much I care, although my actions don't always show it. I do love you and think you're beautiful, charming, delightful, sweet, loving, and a wonderful person to be married to.

Thank you for the children, home and loving care you give me. Thank you for putting up so well with my moods and gripes. Thank you for marrying me and for 18 years of happiness.

My desire is to make you happy and may you have a wonderful Christmas and a healthy, happy new year. May the Lord bless you and keep you—for me—may He continue to give the patience and grace you need to put up with me. In 1965, I'll try to do better and warrant your love and thoughtfulness.

Oceans of Love,

Yours Always,
Honey (me)

Joan and I had many wonderful years together. We would have celebrated our 65th wedding anniversary in 2011. March 9, 1946—wow, that is a day to remember—a day God blessed me, and Joan became my wife. After 64 wonderful years, I came to realize this was no accident! Joan was a gift from God. I miss her very much, but what a peace we can have for those of us who trust in the Lord and know that good-bye is not forever.

Andy Horner
November, 2011

COUNT IT ALL JOY

"And we know that in all things God works
for the good of those who love Him, who have
been called according to His purpose."

ROMANS 8:28

COUNT IT ALL JOY

One of my favorite Bible verses is Nehemiah 8:10: "The joy of the Lord is your strength." You know, happiness is a choice and it can pass away, but joy abides and gives us strength.

We read in Proverbs 17:22 that "a joyful heart is good medicine." Most of us have heard that verse, but there's another one in Proverbs I want to call to your attention: "A joyful heart makes a cheerful face, but when the heart is sad, the spirit is broken" (Proverbs 15:13). Isn't that the truth? A joyful heart is contagious. No one enjoys being around a person whose spirit is broken. Do you have joy? The Biblical example of having contagious joy is right there for us to read and understand.

2001 National Rally

Those of you who have received a note from me know that I like to sign off with the words "Count it all joy!" It's a reminder to me, even as I write, that no matter the circumstance, the joy of the Lord is my strength.

National Rally, 2001

IN ALL THINGS GIVE THANKS

*I*n the next few days we will celebrate our national day of Thanksgiving. This is the time that we say to our family and friends, "Happy Thanksgiving!" That's just the way it should be whenever we are giving thanks—we should feel happy. My friend Mary Crowley always used to say, "You cannot be grateful and unhappy at the same time." How true that is.

We are all familiar with the story of the first Thanksgiving. The arrival of the Pilgrims at Plymouth is well documented in our history books. After a very hard and difficult winter, the Pilgrims buried in the frozen soil of Massachusetts half of those who had come with them. They struggled with extreme weather, illness and loneliness in a strange land. But amidst these struggles, they planted seeds and when harvest time came, they reaped abundantly. One November day they gathered together to give thanks to God. The local Native Americans joined them to celebrate. It was out of this first Thanksgiving that a mighty nation rose. Out of this struggling beginning was built the greatest civilization in the history of mankind.

Our forefathers had a great faith in a sovereign God. They relied on Him to help them handle their challenges. That same God is here for us today. Perhaps looking back over this last year, if you've had some hard times (your own tough "winter"), you can relate to the Pilgrims. Do you show gratitude for the harvest time? Is your heart filled with thanksgiving? Or are you unhappy and ungrateful? Do you realize there is power in giving thanks— power in being grateful?

In the Bible, Paul tells us to "give thanks in all circumstances, for this is God's will for you" (1 Thessalonians 5:18). In Romans 8:28 we read, "We know that God causes everything to work together for the good of those who love God, to those who are called according to His purpose." So, when we understand that word "everything," it puts a different light on it, doesn't it? We can now read 1 Thessalonians 5:18 something like this: "No matter what happens, because God is causing everything to work together for the good of believers, we are always to be thankful, because this is God's will for us."

What makes us thankful? It isn't what's in our pocketbooks, but what's in our hearts.

Update, November 2008

RECIPE FOR JOY

J used to collect old cookbooks, some a hundred years old or more. It's a real joy for me to read them once in a while because they make me laugh. I found a recipe for a "Joyful Day" in one of them and wanted to share it with you. Here are the ingredients:

❧ One relationship with God

❧ One half cup of gratefulness

❧ A sprinkling of songs in your heart

❧ A heaping spoonful of prayer

❧ A tablespoon of children's giggles

❧ A dollop of humor

❧ A dash of sunshine when possible

❧ One pair of rose-colored glasses

Directions: The bottom layer is our relationship with God—this makes a strong base. Then we add gratitude, songs and prayer. Mix thoroughly. Next, fold in giggles, humor and sunshine. Bake overnight with a good night's sleep. Serve with a cheerful attitude and joyful determination, wearing rose-colored glasses to dim the gray skies. This recipe will feed hungry hearts—from one to millions.

Regional Rally, 2010

STRING OF PEARLS

$\mathcal{I}$ want you to make a mental list of some of the things that irritate you. Here are a few suggestions that will get you started. Traffic jams, nosy people, long lines, crying babies, phone calls, misplaced keys, stuck zippers, cold soup, interruptions, nine out of 10 no-shows at a Home Show, noisy neighbors, being rushed, late planes, flat tires, weeds, postponed Home Shows. Any of those irritate you?

There was a funny saying around a few years ago that some of you might identify with: "I am planning to have a nervous breakdown. I have earned it. I deserve it. I have worked hard for it, and nobody's going to keep me from having it." If it weren't for all these irritations, we'd have no problem being patient, would we? Everything in life would be smooth sailing. Unfortunately, life isn't like that. We will never be free of irritations. The secret is to adjust. It's not as easy as it sounds though, is it? But through these adjustments we can have real growth of our inner character; we are able to cultivate attractive qualities.

A perfect illustration of this truth is the oyster and its pearl. Pearls have always been a favorite item of jewelry for women of all ages, economic circumstances, and nationalities. My first piece of jewelry was a tiny string of pearls.

Do you know that something as lovely as a pearl is really a product of irritation? When the shell of an oyster gets pierced and an alien substance, like a grain of sand, slips inside, all the resources within the tiny, sensitive oyster rush to the spot and begin to release healing fluids. By and by, the irritant is covered, and the wound is healed—with a pearl—a tiny jewel conceived through irritation, born of adversity, nursed by adjustments. There could have been no pearl if there had been no wounding, no irritating interruption. Some oysters are never wounded, and those are tossed aside, fit only for oyster stew. That's not all bad, but it's not as good as being fit for Premier pearls.

When I speak of Premier pearls here, I am not only speaking of our jewelry items. I am also referring to each one of you, our Jewelers. We all have had irritants slip inside our lives. For some unknown reason, all the resources within us rush to that spot of stress and pain. What happens then determines if we have a string of pearls or oyster stew.

Let's take one of those irritants I mentioned earlier—a postponed Home Show. What happens when that irritant enters? We can perceive it as a negative, saying "I just knew she wouldn't have the show. I'm not going to bother with her again"—and have oyster stew. Or, we can call that Hostess and say, "I just can't wait until we can set up another date for your show. I have so many new pieces of jewelry and I know that together we're going to hold a great show for you." That's making a string of pearls.

Do you recall all the beautiful, precious stones that are named in the description of the heavenly city in the Bible? Do you remember the entrance to the city? There are 12 gates, which are 12 pearls, the symbol of healed wounds. In the book of James we read what we could call our "pearl verses." Listen to what it says: "When all kinds of trials crowd into our lives, don't resent them as intruders, but welcome them as friends. Realize that they have come to test your endurance. But let the process go on until that endurance is fully developed and you will find you have become men and women of mature character" (James 1:2-4).

As we wear our pearls and show Premier's beautiful strings of pearls to others, I hope we will be reminded of the process we all go through. As we endure adversity, adjust to irritation and recover from misfortune, we become even more beautiful Premier pearls ourselves.

Roundup, approximately 1989

Don't Worry

My friend and mentor, Mary Crowley, once said to me, "We use up today's grace worrying about our tomorrows. God gives us grace for today and for tomorrow—when tomorrow gets here."

> We cannot change yesterday,
>   that is quite clear;
> Nor begin tomorrow until it is here.
> So all that is left for you and for me
> Is to make today the best that can be.

It is sad when we let concerns about our past and worries about our future rob us of our present.

LEARN TO LAUGH AT YOURSELF

One of the strongest unifying elements in our family life has been the gift of laughter. For some of us Horners, it has taken some time to laugh at ourselves. For others of us, it is true pleasure to cause the laughter at another's

2010 Regional Rally

expense. As you get busier with daily chores in a family, it is easy to forget to smile and to laugh! Zig Ziglar said, "The most destitute person in the world is the one without a smile." Look for the fun—not the drab—look for the sun—not the clouds!

We're told this story is true, and I believe it to be so. But whether it is fact or make-believe, the point it makes is about learning to laugh at yourself (and perhaps a reminder of why gossip is bad).

In the days after World War II, English Prime Minister Winston Churchill was found attending an official ceremony in London. Sitting behind him were two men who recognized the statesman. Shaking their heads in disdain, they began whispering between themselves about the politician sitting in front of them.

"They say Churchill's quite senile now," whispered one.

"Yes, they say he's doing England more harm than good," the other whispered back.

"They say he should step aside and leave the running of this government to younger, more dynamic people," continued the first man.

Then, quite abruptly, their malicious gossip ceased when old Churchill turned around and roared, "They also say he's quite deaf!"

Learn to laugh at yourself! Studies have shown many interesting facts about laughing:

- ❀ Laughter reduces stress.

- ❀ Laughter is good exercise, stimulating both abdominal and facial muscles.

- ❀ Laughter stimulates the immune system.

- ❀ Laughter strengthens your lungs.

- ❀ Laughter is an effective treatment for depression.

- ❀ Laughter stimulates creative thinking.

Laughter is contagious. Are you a carrier?

Regional Rally, 2010

THANKS-LIVING

I am reminded of a newly-coined word that one of my former Sunday school teachers once used—*thanks-living*. If we lived up to what that word portrays, we would be giving thanks daily, wouldn't we? It wouldn't just be a once-a-year Thanksgiving holiday affair. The spirit of thanksgiving would linger in our hearts every day.

Psalm 92:1-2 says, "It is good to give thanks to the Lord and to sing praises to Your name, O Most High; to declare Your lovingkindness in the morning and Your faithfulness by night." Now this is quite a task for a Christian mother, but at the same time, it is a wonderful task for us. In the morning, speak of God's lovingkindness and talk about His faithfulness every night.

For many years we had our family devotions in the evening. But as the months went by, our evening meal became more rushed and hectic to the point that we were ready to abandon it. But Andy and I were determined to have it and morning seemed the only other time we were all together. I'm not particularly fond of rising early, but I knew it would be good to start our day together giving thanks.

I once read a story about General George Patton of the American Third Army. He often went out of his way to minister to his men. However, only one ever bothered to write him a letter of appreciation. Think of it! In 35 years of service, only one word of gratitude. Parents have to constantly remind their children after they have received some gift, "Now, Johnnie, what do you say?" Our heavenly Father, too, often waits in vain for our thanks. Do we ever tell our children, "Now, Johnnie, what do you say to God for that blessing?"

The Bible tells us we should give thanks in everything, "for this is the will of God in Christ Jesus concerning you" (1 Thessalonians 5:18). In that early morning hour together, my family can praise God and honor Him. We can share thankful experiences together. Perhaps we have asked for help in some area and the Lord graciously helped us. Isn't it just good manners for us and for our children to thank Him? Teaching our children a simple lesson in daily thanksgiving will not return void to our own lives. We cannot help but learn the lesson ourselves—to become more thankful to the One who gives us all things, and to live a life of daily thanksgiving. That's *thanks-living*.

Talk to Church Women's Group in Gladewater, Texas, 1963

THE LET GO AND LET GOD STORY

A story is told about a mountain climber who wanted to climb the highest mountain. The mountain climber began his adventure after many years of preparation. Wanting all of the glory for himself, he decided to climb the mountain alone. The nights fell heavy in the heights of the mountain and the man could not see anything. All was black. The moon and the stars were covered by the clouds. Zero visibility.

As he climbed higher, only a few feet away from the top of the mountain, he slipped and fell at great speed into thin air. The climber could only see black spots as he went down and felt the terrible sensation of being sucked by gravity. He kept falling, and in those moments of regret and fear, all of the good and bad episodes of his life came to his mind. He realized how close death was approaching, when all of a sudden he felt the rope tied to his waist pull him very hard. His body was hanging in the air with only the rope holding him, and in that moment of stillness he had no other choice but to scream, "Help me, God!"

All of a sudden a deep voice coming from the sky answered, "What do you want me to do?"

"Save me, God!!"

"Do you really think I can save you?"

The climber answered, "Of course I believe You can."

"Then cut the rope that is tied to your waist."

There was a moment of silence as the man thought about what to do. He decided to hold on to the rope with all his strength.

The next day, the rescue team reported that the climber was found dead and frozen. His body was hanging from a rope, his frozen hands holding tightly to it … only 10 feet from the ground.

And what about you and me? How attached are we to our ropes? Will you let go? Will I? Don't ever doubt the things from God. You never should say that He has forgotten or abandoned you. Don't ever think that God does not take care of you. Remember that He is always holding on to you. He promises, "I hold you by your right hand. I, the Lord your God. And I say to you, 'Do not be afraid. I am here to help you' " (Isaiah 41:13).

One of Joan's Favorite Stories

Don't Lose Hope

I cannot count the number of letters we receive telling us how people have gained new hope through Premier Designs. All of us need hope—hope for health, hope for income to raise a family, hope for friends. We hope for so many things, some of which can be found in and through Premier Designs. Some people are lonely without family. Maybe hope for them is the Premier family, who are waiting with open hearts.

We don't know the future, of course, but we do know Who holds the future. We must not give up. We must pray and love and hold one another up with hope.

GOD HAS PLANS FOR YOU

*I*n the Old Testament, we read about a time when the little southern kingdom of Judah was on the brink of disaster, threatened by mighty Babylon. God called Jeremiah, His prophet, to encourage His people to submit to Babylon's domination as the Lord's discipline. But they were not to lose hope. If Judah surrendered to Babylon, God promised to protect them from being destroyed or taken captive. Then eventually, if Judah turned from its sin and back to God, God promised to restore the nation to independence again. Jeremiah's message was plain and simple: obey, believe, hope, and return to the Lord.

Jeremiah, known as the weeping prophet, was a lone voice for most of his ministry. He lived under kings who had no regard for morality, let alone regard for God. He kept on preaching for 40 years, even when he was rejected by family, friends, and neighbors. What kept Jeremiah going? I think it was hope.

Hope meant to try it one more time—to preach one more sermon. Maybe this time they would believe. If you have ever planted a seed, you know the power and promise of hope. One more day and you might see fruit! Jeremiah recorded these words right from the Lord: "For I know the plans I have for you," declares the Lord, "plans to prosper you and not to harm you, plans to give you hope and a future" (Jeremiah 29:11). What a promise for you and me! God knows His plans for Premier. We do not. He said His plans are for good and not for evil.

"Oh, really? Well, He's not talking about me," you say. "I can't get bookings any more, and that's not good, is it?" Or you say, "I was a Designer and lost all my first-level. Don't tell me that's good." Hold on just a minute and listen to the rest of the story. The "plans" God talks about—His plans—are to give us a future and a hope.

Your future in this business depends on bookings. There is somebody out there who needs to hostess a Home Show. Hold on to that hope, and make just one more call. Just ask one more person. Work and hope go together. But remember—don't hope more than you work.

That future Hostess, in God's plans, needs hope, too. So many people out there need hope. They need hope, first of all, in the One who gives hope—God Himself. Then they need hope to provide for their families, hope to be able to stay at home with young children, hope for their future.

Martin Luther said, "Everything that is done in the world is done by hope." To modernize that idea a little, we could say: Hope is to dreams what baking powder is to biscuits; or, hope is taking along a camera when you go fishing!

God has a plan for each of us; a plan for a future and a hope. When you trust in God's good plans for you, you will become a person who reaches out with hope. People love that human touch—a warm hug or just a friendly pat on the back. Do your part in passing on hope. This is fulfilling Premier's purpose of enriching lives.

National Rally, 1998

Three Essentials

The three great essentials of happiness are:

1 Something to Do (*We can go into the homes of America and give hope.*)

2 Someone to Love (*We can go into the homes of America and give love.*)

3 Something to Hope For (*Through Premier you can fulfill your own dreams and find God's purpose in your life.*)

Our wonderful Father in heaven gives us all three of these opportunities in Premier to choose our happiness.

The Cat from Heaven Story

This is a cute story that I heard actor and author Jeannette Clift George tell many times. It's about her cousin, Jesse, who doesn't like cats, and his wife, Frances, who does.

One day a little neighbor girl ran crying to Jesse and Frances's house. Her cat had climbed up in a tall slender tree and couldn't get down. Jesse thought that was a very good place for a cat to be, but following Frances's gentle persuasion, he said, "Let's see what we can do to help." The two of them decided that Frances, who is quite petite, would grab the lower part of the tree and pull it down gradually until the top most branches reached Jesse. Then Jesse, who is quite tall, would scoop the frightened cat from the top of the tree to safety.

Their plan worked well at first. Frances grabbed the part of the tree within her reach and pulled it toward her. The tree tipped down like a thirsty giraffe, with the cat hanging on tightly. The branches were almost to Jesse when Frances lost her grip! WHOOM! The tree slipped from Frances's hands and sprang away with such great force that the cat was flung into space! The little girl cried even louder and Frances was overcome by guilt, because she and Jesse had lost the little girl's cat. Jesse tried hard not to laugh, but what could they do now?

A few days later, Frances was in the grocery store and noticed a friend pushing a grocery cart with cat food in it. She knew her friend's husband didn't like cats any better than Jesse did. "I see you have cat food. Do you have a cat now?" Frances asked. Her friend stopped, looked around to be sure no one else could hear, and said, "Frances, the strangest thing happened! My husband and I were sitting in our backyard, when all of a sudden, out of nowhere this cat landed at our feet. My husband looked at the cat and then at me. He said, "Maude, the Lord has sent us a cat!"

One of Joan's Favorite Stories

LOOK UP

$\mathcal{S}$ometimes we feel very, very small, as though everything in our lives is just too big for us to handle. I saw a cartoon recently that showed what the world looks like to a toddler. Tables and chairs looked as big as skyscrapers. The family car looked like a grizzly bear, and adults amounted to big legs from the knees down. That's an interesting glimpse of what it's like when you're very small and everything around you looms so much bigger.

Some days are like that for adults, too. We can find ourselves under the pile. We can lose our perspective. But God is big enough for any need we have. Ephesians 3:20-21 reminds us of that fact: "Now to Him who is able to do immeasurably more than all we ask or imagine, according to His power that is at work within us, to Him be glory . . . forever and ever!"

Keep looking up, and keep counting it all joy.

Pacesetter, June 1989

KEEP IT PERSONAL

"Finally, brothers and sisters, rejoice! Strive
for full restoration, encourage one another,
be of one mind, live in peace."

2 CORINTHIANS 13:11

KEEPING IT PERSONAL

2007 National Rally

*M*y personal mission in Premier is very simple. I have committed to keeping the culture of Premier on a personal level, from top to bottom and from side to side. My own slogan is one I have held to since we began Premier—*Keep It Personal.* That doesn't just happen, though, does it? We must work at keeping a personal touch in all of our relationships.

There are many ways to keep it personal. Here are some of my favorites.

❀ **PERSONAL CONTACT:** We need to enjoy each other's company face to face. We need to spend time together.

❀ **PERSONAL PHONE CALLS:** So much is communicated by hearing someone's voice. I am sure you have all heard volumes of meaning hidden in someone's words. My friends will say, "You sound so tired today," or "Wow, you must have had a wonderful day," or "Is something going on? I can tell by your voice." We can hear so much on the phone—more than we can in a text message!

❧ **PERSONAL HANDWRITTEN WORDS:** Much can be communicated in handwritten notes. A written note is warm and personal. I will include writing e-mails here. I agree that it is acceptable in a business environment, but I do not believe that e-mails really build personal relationships. What says "you are special and worth my time and my effort" more than a personal, handwritten note? You say, "Well, we can write the same words in an e-mail as we write with a pen." Yes, but somehow feelings and the tone are hidden. I've found that writing from my heart with a pen or pencil is more revealing of how much I care for that person. I don't believe e-mails feel nearly as personal.

Premier Designs is different and unique. When the Southwest Entrepreneur of the Year Award was presented to us in 2004, they made mention of the different business culture that was evident at Premier. That different culture was easy for them to identify—it involved caring and sharing and serving, and *Keeping It Personal*. I am convinced that the difference between Premier and other companies of similar size is that we have a purpose of enriching lives and serving others. What could be more personal than that!

National Rally, 2007

YOU CAN MAKE A DIFFERENCE

*D*o you want to be a person of hope and make a difference in someone's life? There are three easy ways that you can do that using my "see, feel, do" formula: seeing a need, feeling the urge to help, and doing something kind.

There are many needy people out there in Premier. Do you see them? Can you be a friend? It will take a personal connection to give a hug to encourage a lonely person. Do you see someone at your Home Show who really needs what Premier has to offer? Do you see a single mom who needs additional income to pay those mounting bills? Do you see a mother who desperately wants to be at home with her new precious baby? Perhaps a husband is laid off from his job; do you see where Premier could be an answer to their needs?

Next, do you feel that you can help and encourage others? Yes, you can do it. The Bible tells us to comfort and encourage each other (see 1 Thessalonians 4:18). Of course, I don't need to remind us that any encouragement we offer should be very personal, that personal touch. I would like each of you to be a personal encourager—to really feel that you can make a difference. It will sometimes cost a lot of our own personal time. It will not always be convenient. People don't seem to have low times and need help when it is convenient for our schedule. But I do hope we can feel the need to encourage and love on those who are hurting.

We see the need; we feel a desire to help; and finally, we do something about it. This "doing" can come in many forms. We may take a hot meal to someone who is ill and not able to care for her family. Maybe we can help take their young children to the bus for school. We can sit and talk to someone at a Home Show who is sad and lonely. We can make that extra phone call to just check in on that Hostess. You can come up with countless ways, big or small, to do something that will make a difference in someone's life.

Every day there are opportunities to reach out and touch someone. People love that human touch—a friendly pat on the shoulder or a warm hug. Do what you can to pass on hope to others and you will be fulfilling Premier's purpose of enriching lives.

Regional Rally, 2009

WE ALL NEED COMPASSION

2008 National Rally

I have been trying to find a good definition for the word *compassionate*. It is such an all-inclusive word that, in English, it is difficult to really understand it. I think being compassionate means to care about others ahead of ourselves, to be understanding, kind and forgiving. We read in the book of Ephesians, "Get rid of all bitterness, rage, anger, harsh words, and slander, as well as all types of evil behavior. Instead, be kind to each other, tenderhearted, forgiving one another, just as God through Christ has forgiven you" (Ephesians 4:31-32). Compassion includes forgiveness, kindness, tenderness—all of that.

We have ample opportunity to show compassion. So many women come into the Premier family hurting, lonely and desperate for compassion and care. What a blessing for us that we can show that hurting mother, that lonely sister or daughter that there is light at the end of the tunnel; that they are a somebody, because God didn't take time to make a nobody.

I love the saying, "God doesn't love you because you are important; you are important because God loves you." We can pass that message on to all who need compassion, to those who need a tender word. Isn't that thrilling? We can have our own business that encourages us to care for others—to do unto others as we would have others do to us.

National Rally, 2008

Temperature Makes a Difference

My precious pastor of years ago preached one time about changing temperatures. He asked if we knew what was the only difference between the iceberg, which sank the beautiful Titanic, and the beautiful waves on which the Titanic floated. The only difference was the temperature!

Keeping it personal is the warmer temperature in your business! You can do that at your Home Shows. Create a warm atmosphere. Be intentional about keeping that personal touch.

Be an Encourager!

*W*ith the challenges in today's society, we need not look very far to see people who are carrying heavy burdens. Young and old, male and female, no matter the race or religion—problems show up regularly for all of us. Many people have lost confidence and have a low sense of self-worth.

What a good time for the Premier family to step up and encourage others. "Bear one another's burdens," the Bible tells us. And now is a great time to do just that—to show love. To love someone is to be supportive. There are opportunities for all of us in the Premier family to hold each other up. Our Premier "families" should be strong encouragers of those temporarily challenged economically.

Now is our time to "Keep It Personal." Not necessarily in the plural, but one-on-one! Keeping it personal could mean making an investment of time with a friend—giving of our own personal time. It could mean offering to sit with their kids, or sharing training tips, or saying something positive when they are down. However it's done, being an encourager and bearing each other's burdens always means it's not all about us; it's about others.

Regional Rally, 2010

FORGIVENESS AND WORSHIP

*H*ave you ever dug in your heels and insisted on being right and doing things your way? Have you crushed someone's heart and love in the process? The New Testament tells the story of a Pharisee named Simon who struggled with that very thing.

Simon invited Jesus into his house for a meal, when something unexpected happened. Luke records the story for us: "[Jesus] entered the Pharisee's house and reclined at the table. And there was a woman in the city who was a sinner; and when she learned that He was reclining at the table in the Pharisee's house, she brought an alabaster vial of perfume, and standing behind Him at His feet, weeping, she began to wet His feet with her tears, and kept wiping them with the hair of her head, and kissing His feet and anointing them with the perfume" (Luke 7:36-38).

Well, the Pharisee was incensed. He saw himself as being more spiritual than the woman. Luke tells us his secret thoughts: "Now when the Pharisee who had invited [Jesus] saw this, he said to himself, 'If this man were a prophet He would know who and what sort of person this woman is who is touching Him, that she is a sinner'" (Luke 7:39). He didn't say this out loud, but you can imagine how Simon was probably looking down his nose at her, shaming her and crushing her spirit. Has anyone ever crushed your heart and made you feel inadequate or inferior? Jesus has an answer for that.

Knowing what the Pharisee was thinking and what was in his heart, Jesus confronted him. In the Pharisee's mind, the woman was unclean and Jesus was violating the law by allowing her to touch Him. With this assessment came the implication that he always obeyed the law; that he, a Pharisee, was right before God. Speaking to his arrogance, Jesus pitted the Pharisee's confidence in being righteous against the woman's heart that believed in God for forgiveness and wanted to worship Him.

Jesus told Simon that He had something to say to him, and the Pharisee replied, "Tell me, Teacher." Fortunately, he had the humility to listen, unlike some people, who are so sure of themselves that they can only hear themselves talk. Jesus said, "I entered your house and you gave Me no water for My feet, but she has wet My feet with her tears and wiped them with her hair. You gave Me no kiss, but she, since the time I came in, has not ceased to kiss My feet. You did not anoint My head with oil, but she anointed My feet with perfume" (Luke 7:44-46).

Jesus showed Simon that while he was focusing on being right and not needing forgiveness for anything, he totally missed the fact that he, too, was a sinner. Meanwhile, the woman recognized her sinfulness and worshiped God extravagantly because she was overwhelmed with gratitude to her Savior.

God wants pure worship from a heart that simply says, "If this pleases you, Lord, let me pour out my life, my time, and my greatest treasures at your feet, simply as an act of worship, and not because there is some rate of return." Be careful not to argue against worship with human reasoning. Just know that God is deserving of our extravagant worship.

I wonder if God is asking for our extravagant worship in some way today—in the way we love those around us, and in the way we love Him.

Found on Joan's desk in early 2011

Send a Note

You may think that because your Premier mother is a Three Diamond Designer or your Premier grandmother is a Five Diamond Designer that they've arrived and have it all together. Not so! They need encouragement, too. Send them a happy note once in a while and tell them they are appreciated. Remember, they have needs, too.

THE ART OF FRIENDSHIP

One thing I have discovered is that the Bible stresses *being* a friend while our emphasis seems to be on *having* friends. But in order to have friends, we first have to be a friend. What does that mean? Proverbs 17:17 says, "A friend loves

1988 Rally

at all times." A true friend, then, continues to love and to show that love whatever the circumstances. Being a friend is active, taking the initiative.

Our Premier family is a wonderful school for learning the art of friendship. We can be a real help in time of need. We can accept people for who and what they are. We can be a consistent encourager, a loyal advisor, and a faithful supporter. Remember that a talk with a friend is sweeter than a bottle of Chanel No. 5!

Pacesetter, July 1988

Shine the Light

We are called to carry the light—our light of service—into the homes of America. Let your light shine by your good works, your encouraging words, your listening ear; by working with your new Jeweler, helping a Hostess when she is discouraged, writing encouraging notes not only to your downline, but also to your upline. Carry your light and keep it personal by sharing, caring and giving—and doing it all for God's glory.

LISTENING WITH YOUR HEART

One of the biggest complaints that teenagers have of their parents is, "They don't listen to me." There have been many books written about the art of listening. How are you at listening?

I am so grateful that God listens to us. He promises, "Call to me and I will answer you" (Jeremiah 33:3). He is never too busy. I can call on God anytime and He listens. I am so glad God never has said to me, "Joan, I am too busy right now to listen." No, my heavenly Father listens!

There's a story about a girl who was in college. She had two problems very common to many students—low grades and no money. She had to come up with some way of communicating this to her parents, and do it in a positive way so they would listen to her! So, she wrote them a letter:

Dear Mom and Dad,

Just thought I'd drop you a note to clue you in on my plans. I've fallen in love with a guy named Jim. He quit high school after grade eleven to get married. About a year ago he got a divorce. We've been going steady for two months and I plan to move into his apartment. I think I might be pregnant. At any rate, I dropped out of school last week, although I would like to finish college sometime in the future.

On the next page she continued:

> Mom and Dad, I just want you to know that everything I've written so far in this letter is false. None of it is true. But, it is true that I got a C in French and flunked math. And it is true that I'm going to need some more money for my tuition payments.

That is a pretty sharp co-ed! I think her parents probably listened to her. What do you think?

How are we as listeners? Proverbs 18:13 says this: "What a shame—what folly—to give advice before listening to the facts." This verse is referring to a person who does not know how to listen. Have you ever thought about what it requires to really listen to another person?

Most of us are so busy that much of the time we only hear the noise. We are not hearing with our hearts, so we're not really listening. We may hear the sound, but the message of the words doesn't enter our hearts, which says to that person that we really don't care all that much.

One of my special memories is when I met George W. Bush back when he was the managing president of the Texas Rangers, long before politics got in the way. My son Tim and I were selecting our suite before the new ballpark was finished. During our time there, George W. walked in and spent a lot of his valuable time with us, helping us to make a good decision as to the location of our suite, and other details. When he was speaking to us, he never took his eyes off our eyes. That told us immediately that we mattered to him. His attention was a very important part of listening. You can have all the wisdom in the world, but unless, and until, people believe you have heard them, your words of wisdom will fall on deaf ears.

It is so important to be a good listener in building relationships. Listening is very important in nurturing our children, and in building a strong love-filled, harmonious marriage. Think for a moment about people in your life who have had the most positive impact since you were a little child. I would imagine it would be the person who paid attention to what you were saying and who looked you right in the eyes. That is the person we long remember. Let's listen to those who train us. Listen to our Hostesses. Listen to our customers. And then listen to that still small voice of God.

If we really listen with our hearts, I believe we will be better servants and, I think, better leaders. And I know we will be better persons.

Roundup, 2010

Be a Good Teammate

Life itself is a team sport, and all of us need occasional pats on the back from our teammates. Whether you realize it or not, many people with whom you come in contact every day are in desperate need of a smile or an encouraging word. Since we don't always know who needs our help, the best thing to do is to try to encourage all the people we interact with, as well as those we just see as passersby.

THE PERFECT WORDS STORY

Here's a story that illustrates beautifully the power of our words:

Carl was driving to work one morning when he bumped fenders with another motorist. Both cars stopped, and the woman driving the other car got out to survey the damage. She was distraught. It was her fault, she admitted, and hers was a new car, less than two days from the showroom. She dreaded facing her husband. Carl was sympathetic, but he had to pursue the exchange of license and registration date. She reached into her glove compartment to retrieve the documents in an envelope. On the first paper to tumble out, written in her husband's distinctive hand, were these words: "In case of accident, remember, Honey, it's you I love—not the car."

What a perfect note. What complete love.

One of Joan's Favorite Stories

Be a True Friend

*M*ost of you know that keeping relationships personal is a passion of mine. This is how *Webster's Dictionary* defines the word *personal*: "of, or peculiar to, a certain person, individual; done in person or by oneself without the use of another person or outside agency; having the character and personality of a certain person." The various meanings of this word are interesting, and underneath it all is relationship—friendship—giving of yourself to others.

Friendships require maintenance. You must value that personal relationship above just about anything else. When our strength fails and illness comes, when we have no shows lined up, when we grow weary and discouraged—that's when we need a friend to come alongside to show understanding and compassion. When the bills pile up and money runs short, we need an encouraging friend. It takes time, but it's worth it.

Be a friend to someone you don't know quite as well as you'd like; or better still, be a real friend to those you do know well and perhaps have taken for granted.

Talk given at a women's retreat, 2006

Heartwarming Notes

I love writing personal notes and I also love receiving them. I have long encouraged people to write handwritten notes. Whether it is a quick thank-you, a needed word of encouragement, or a pouring out of your soul, there is such a friendly, heartwarming feel when you send and when you receive handwritten words. To be very honest, I rarely feel warmed by e-mails I receive. The words just are not speaking to me personally. Give me a handwritten note anytime. Nothing is more personal than that.

LOVE AND FAMILY

"Love is patient, love is kind ... It does not dishonor
others, it is not self-seeking, it is not easily angered,
it keeps no record of wrongs ... It always protects,
always trusts, always hopes, always perseveres."

1 CORINTHIANS 13:4-7

ONE BIG HAPPY FAMILY

What is a family? Two parents and children. One parent and children. Grandparents and grandchildren. A family is any blend of people and it is designed for the growth of those within the family. It is a center for developing and nurturing values, attitudes, beliefs, creativity, and most of all character. The family is society's most important institution. It prepares children for life. It lays the foundation for their character.

The apostle Peter talks about how Christians should behave. "You should be like one big happy family, full of sympathy toward each other, loving one another with tender hearts and humble minds. Don't repay evil for evil. Don't snap back at those who say unkind things about you. Instead, pray for God's help for them, for we are to be kind to others, and God will bless us for it" (1 Peter 3:8-9). "One big happy family," it says. Our families aren't always happy every hour and every second of the day, of course; but if we are kind, it goes a long way.

Proverbs 16:24 says, "Kind words are like honey—enjoyable and healthy." Kind words help build a happy family. Another proverb says, "A happy face means a glad heart" (Proverbs 15:13). A happy face instead of a sad one. "A cheerful heart does good like medicine" (Proverbs 17:22). Cheerful, smiling, kind. These expressions go a long way to building happy families.

Peter said we should be full of sympathy. Sympathy is a feeling of caring. It is manifested in bearing one another's burdens. And I think it shows itself most in listening. Listening to each other is a vital link in any family unit. Once we start listening to another person, we will begin to put ourselves in the other person's shoes, and then sympathy becomes automatic.

So, we are to be one big happy family, full of sympathy, and "loving one another with tender hearts and humble minds." You have heard it said, "Houses are made of wood and stone, but only love can make a home." We all need tender love, gentle love, humble love. What does that kind of love look like? The famous "Love Chapter" in 1 Corinthians 13 tells us that love is patient. It's willing to wait. Love does not envy. It's happy for the others in the family. It does not boast. It is not proud or rude or easily angered. Love protects, trusts, hopes, and perseveres. And there's no defensiveness or retaliation in happy families. "Don't repay evil for evil," Peter reminds us. Don't snap back at those who say unkind words about you. Instead, pray for them.

How does this apply to Premier Designs? Well, our Home Office team is a family unit, of sorts. We who work here must show each other that we care and will listen, and we must be kind to one another, and love each other. I owe it to my Home Office family to do my very best, to be trusting and trustworthy. And who cares who gets the credit?

1988 Rally

Every Premier downline is a "family" unit, too. And if the family units fail, Premier will fail. It's the most important in-stitution in Premier. Can you have a big happy Premier family? Yes, absolutely! One with smiles, not frowns. With compliments instead of complaints. With kind words, not gossip. With patience instead of envy or pride or retaliation. With trust and hope and prayer. With these things, you will be one big, happy family.

National Rally, 1988

Three Little Words

One Scripture verse I encouraged my own children to memorize when they were young is Ephesians 4:32, "Be ye kind one to another, tenderhearted, forgiving one another, even as God for Christ's sake has forgiven you." Three little words—kind, tenderhearted, forgiving—become three huge words in family life. They are also helpful words in your business "family." Guard your own family and your Premier family, too. Live with kindness, tenderheartedness and forgiveness.

WHAT IS A FAMILY?

This is the 81st year I have lived in a family. I lived in a family first as a baby and child, and now as a mother, grandmother, and great-grandmother. This year is my 61st year as a wife and my 59th year as a mother. What is a family? It is all of these changing and growing relationships.

I believe all of us want to be part of a family. Each one of us longs for relationships in a close environment. When we began Premier Designs, the different levels were referred to as parts of a "family." Is that significant, do you think? Building your business by building a "family"? That was our desire from the very beginning—to build a strong Premier family that enriches lives, serves other and honors God.

Everyone begins life as a child of someone; that's our entry into the family. We enter with huge needs. We need food. We need to be warm. We need our personal needs tended to and our diapers kept dry. As our needs are met, we respond in a positive way.

Then, the child grows up, marries, and has a child of her own. Now her role in the family has become very different. The mother now has the responsibility of providing the food. She is responsible for the warmth and comfort of her child. As the child grows, the needs are larger and must be met in order for the child to grow to maturity. As the child's needs are met, he or she will respond in a positive way.

And, in time, we may become a grandmother or beyond. In Premier, without mothers and grandmothers and great-grand-mothers, we would not have a company!

Let's look at two things a mother can and must do for her children—those she has birthed or adopted, as well as ones she has sponsored into her Premier family.

TEACH YOUR CHILDREN. The Bible says, "You must commit yourselves wholeheartedly to these commands that I am giving you today. Repeat them again and again to your children. Talk about them when you are at home and when you are on the road, when you are going to bed and when you are getting up" (Deuteronomy 6:6-7) Pretty clear, isn't it? Parents are to teach their children. Proverbs 22:6 is another great principle for parents. It says, "Train up a child in the way he should go, and when he is old, he will not depart from it." That is God's Word. Teach and train your children.

Teach and train those you sponsor. Teach them one-by-one. A new Jeweler deserves the best from her mother. Take the time to show her how to book shows, teach her the elements of a good

Home Show, train her with the Jeweler's Handbook, teach her that she is Premier. If you train up your Jewelers, they will remain faithful, loyal Jewelers for a long time.

❦ LOVE YOUR CHILDREN. You may say, "Well, that's a given." But not necessarily. We see and read of terrible abuses of children who are not loved by their parents. Titus 2:4 says, "Older women must train the younger women to love their husbands and their children." This is a huge message to all of us. Andy often has said that the husband you take on the honeymoon is not the same one you bring home! You must learn to love him, and learn how to show him that you do. And it's the same with children. We must learn to love them, and how to show that love.

This carries over into your Premier family. Show love to your new Jeweler, even if sometimes that love must be learned.

Designer Conference, 2007

TRUST AND FORGIVENESS

Trust is so important. A family needs trust to be a great family. No marriage can be called a good one unless there is total trust between the husband and wife. You have to trust your partner to be faithful, honest, understanding and kind. The partner must be trustworthy in all these and many other areas of living. That trust is applied to your children also.

Trust in your employer or your business partner is very important, too. You must have trust in the management of our company—trust in decisions that are made that affect you as a Jeweler, whether you agree or not. Are you able to build a healthy trust relationship with your upline and downline? Maybe you think that is not so important, but it is! People will naturally befriend others whom they can trust. Trust is the glue that holds relationships together, whether it is in a family, a career, or a relationship with God.

If trust is broken, we must choose to forgive. To have a successful marriage, there has to be forgiveness of both small and large hurts, offering your spouse a second chance, a third chance, a fiftieth chance—forgive up to "seventy times seven," we are told by Jesus (Matthew 18:22). In our Premier family settings, there are dozens and dozens of opportunities to forgive—every day!

The following is an amazing example of forgiveness:

Mr. Meck, a Pennsylvania farmer, had a wonderful wife and a darling little boy. When the boy was old enough to attend school, he eagerly waited for the bus each morning. Each afternoon the family waited for him to arrive home.

One day the school bus was stopped on the road, with its warning lights flashing. A driver failed to heed the lights and rammed into the bus. The Meck's little boy was instantly killed. Losing a child that way is probably the worst sorrow human beings can feel. The Mecks were devastated.

Angry friends urged them to sue the careless driver. Yet, grieved though they were, the Mecks knew that the driver was suffering, too. They prayed about their situation, and as they prayed they knew what they had to do. They invited the driver and his wife to dinner. After several awkward moments for both couples, Mr. Meck said, "We have prayed for strength to forgive you, and God has given us an answer. We offer you forgiveness."

That would be tough, wouldn't it? Forgiveness like that is offered only at special times, but forgiveness on any level is necessary to keep marriages healthy and to build strong relationships in our families and businesses.

Regional Rally, 2010

MOTHERS ARE INVESTORS

*O*ften, when I am introduced to someone for the first time, they will ask me, "What do you do?" Many years ago, as a young mom, that question tended to irritate me. I guess the irritation worked in me as it does in the oyster shell, because now the "pearl" comes forward in me. Instead of being irritated, I am proud to answer, "I am Andy's wife," or "I am Andrea, Sarah, Tim, Mary and Tommy's mother." This is my title: wife and mother. Mothers have always been a priority in Premier Designs. I'd like to pay tribute to all our Premier Moms. You are very special to us.

A mother's most important job, and the one with the greatest rewards, is her work with her children. Your children are your investment! Don't you want to experience what the writer of Proverbs 31:28 says? "Her children arise up, and call her blessed; her husband also and he praiseth her." Here are some ways I've found to be an investor in the lives of your children.

First, invest in them spiritually, by teaching them God's Word from early on. Take care of their spiritual needs first. Make sure they know that Jesus loves them.

Second, invest in them physically, by taking care of their bodies. Try to provide regular nourishing meals for them (not McDonald's every other night!). If they are interested in sports activities, encourage them by attending their games. And of course, we could all benefit by exercising regularly with our children.

Finally, invest in your children emotionally. They need lots of love, hugs and compliments. Remember, these "little people" need an investor who sees the opportunity to train her children as a very profitable one. Not for financial profit, but for the promise of a godly life bringing glory and honor to our heavenly Father.

Update, May 2007

Parent Time

No one can take your place. God is counting on you to be involved in the lives of your children. Let them know they are special to you by spending time and showing up. Never let them think you have less interest in them just because you have an exciting career.

LOVE AND FRIENDSHIP

*W*ithout love there is no happiness in a family, a business partnership or a marriage. But friendship is equally important, I believe. Friendship is being totally comfortable with each other. Friendship and love

2010 Regional Rally

together are the basis of all strong relationships. To have one without the other weakens the relationship.

In Premier, these two qualities exist side by side. Love strengthens friendship and friendship strengthens love. Those who are friends need to learn what it means to love more deeply, and those who love can take a strong look at the friendship link in a marriage or in a business relationship. As family members grow together, they learn to be friends and to love each other, though not always in that order.

Regional Rally, 2010

BALANCING ACT

Many of you are double mothers. You're a mom with children at home *and* a Premier "mom" with Jewelers in your downline. It is important to us that you are fulfilled in your role as a wife and mother at home, as well as in your business. That requires balance.

There are some great illustrations in the Bible of the need for balance. Remember the story about Moses in Exodus 18:13-23? He was sitting, as usual, to hear and judge the people's complaints about each other. They were lined up from morning to evening. Jethro, his father-in-law, asked him why he was doing that all by himself. Moses replied that he was the *only one* who could do the job! Ever been there? I have!

Jethro said, "This is not good! You're going to wear yourself out—and the people too. This job is too heavy a burden for you to handle all by yourself." Moses may not have liked hearing that, but Jethro was wise. He went on, "It is too much for you to do alone. My advice is to find others to help you to serve the people. The really important jobs can be handled by you alone."

Moses' life was out of balance. His work consumed all of his time, and he was pretty defensive about it. "Well, the people call on me all the time . . . they need me!" He was trying to justify his out-of-balance life. But his father-in-law wasn't buying it. Jethro said in so many words: "Call for help." That was the only way Moses would be there for the long haul.

What about you? What about me? Do we want to be part of Premier Designs for the long haul? If so, then balance is so important. We need balance between family and work. Our Premier business can't be allowed to destroy our marriages or our families. Some of you might say, "Well, my kids are little now. It will get easier when they are teenagers." Wrong! There is never an age while your children are in your home that they don't need their parents.

For those of you who do have children in the home, I'd like to suggest some ideas to get you thinking about the problem of balance. You husbands and wives can get together and discuss it, and come up with ideas of your own.

❦ THE OFFICE IS NOT OPEN DURING MEAL TIME. No telephone calls or e-mails. You may tell your downline that there will be times you are off-line, and that you will get back to them as soon as you are able. I think it is rude to be talking on the phone or checking messages during meal time. Not only are we setting poor examples of balanced lives to our downlines, but we are saying to our spouses and children that they don't have our full attention. For me, the same courtesy should be paid to your children when they get home from school. Give them some of your undivided attention and time.

❋ HAVE A CALENDAR BOOK JUST FOR YOUR CHILDREN. Be creative and let them help you make their own date book. Keep it in a very special place that they choose for themselves. Then, you and your children together put in the dates for their activities that you will attend. Be sure to keep close tabs on this calendar, and be available for the special events. Who knows, as they get older, maybe they'll become JITs—Jewelers in Training. Then they'll be part of both of your families!

❋ MAKE IT A PRIORITY TO BE AVAILABLE TO YOUR HUSBAND. Maybe have a date night or a date breakfast. Work together on that. Lord willing, you'll have many years together after the children have left home, so don't neglect each other. Cherish each other and make time together.

❋ CONSIDER HIRING HELP IN YOUR HOME. Having someone to do a few household chores (laundry, running errands, cleaning house) will free you up to do those things only you can do. You can also help another person by giving them a job. Maybe you can do two or three more Home Shows a month in order to get help. That frees you up more when you're home to give your attention to your children and husband.

Please realize that you are not Superwoman! By paying attention to the balance in your life, and being disciplined about maintaining that balance, you *can* be a super mom, a super wife, and a super Jeweler. We want you around for the long haul.

Designer Leadership Conference, 2007

What Is It?

It is healthy. It helps the body's immune system. It cures depression. It reduces stress. It induces sleep. It's invigorating. It's rejuvenating. It has no unpleasant side effects.

It is all-natural, organic, naturally sweet and 100-percent wholesome. It contains no pesticides, preservatives or artificial ingredients. There are no movable parts, no batteries to wear out, no periodic checkups, no insurance requirements, and no monthly payments. It is inflation-proof, nonfattening, theftproof, nontaxable, nonpolluting, and fully-returnable.

What is it? It's hugging!

EVERY PART COUNTS

Have you ever thought about how you are made? The psalmist said, "I will give thanks to you, for I am fearfully and wonderfully made" (Psalm 139:14). Well, I am here to attest to that fact! Some of you may know that I recently had a joint in my hand replaced with a new one. (Isn't it sad to wear out?) I just wanted to share some of the neat things I have learned through this experience.

My thumb is one part of my hand, which is one part of my arm, which is attached to my shoulder. When my thumb hurts, my hand is slowed down, my arm is sluggish, and my shoulder feels it. All the parts are interrelated. Paul talked about this: "Yes, the body has many parts for a reason. But if the foot says, 'I am not a part of the body because I am not a hand,' that does not make it any less a part of the body. Suppose the whole body were an eye—then how would you hear? Or if your whole body were just one big ear, how could you smell anything? But that isn't the way God has made us. He has made many parts for our bodies and has put each part just where He wants it" (1 Corinthians 12:14-18).

So from this Scripture passage I learn that my poor sore weak thumb is just as important as my healthy strong foot. All my parts are necessary. The Bible teaches us that Christians belong to the body of Christ, which is symbolic of the unity of each member with the other, just like parts of the human body.

How does that apply to the Premier family? In every way! When one member of the Premier family is hurting, the one next and closest to her hurts, too. When one member of the Premier family is discouraged, not able to book shows or sponsor someone new into the business, then the family member closest is needed to encourage and support. This is what happened while my left thumb was healing—my right hand took the place of my left hand for a few weeks.

A friend told me that after the doctor removes my cast I will probably feel unsupported and insecure, even to the point of wanting the cast put back on. That reminds me of some who are new in the business. They may feel lost and unsupported. They need that "cast" on for security. Maybe you, as a member of her family, can be that "cast."

What if we had all Designers in Premier? Then there would be no families. If everyone in the Home Office did accounting, who would inspect our jewelry? You see, we are designed to complete the whole picture, each part being very important and necessary.

Pacesetter, March, 1987

Success That Counts

We don't count success in numbers alone, but in the lives of people who have been touched and changed forever. I could read you dozens and dozens of testimonies that we receive from stay-at-home moms, dozens more from single moms, and still more from young husbands—all of them testifying that their lives were changed because of their involvement with Premier Designs. Marriages have been strengthened. Single parents are encouraged. And mothers are able to be at home with their young children during those crucial formative years of their lives and still contribute to the family finances. That's the kind of success we are after.

THE GIFT OF YOURSELF STORY

*G*iving of ourselves is a priceless gift. I read a story once that perfectly illustrates what it means to give of ourselves. This is taken from the book *Who Switched the Price Tags?* by Anthony Campolo.

Teddy Stallard certainly qualified as "one of the least." Disinterested in school. Musty, wrinkled clothes. Hair never combed. One of those kids in school with a deadpan face, expressionless—sort of a glassy, unfocused stare. When Miss Thompson spoke to Teddy, he always answered in monosyllables. Unattractive, unmotivated, and distant, he was just plain hard to like. Even though his teacher said she loved all in her class the same, down inside she wasn't being completely truthful.

Whenever she marked Teddy's papers, she got a certain perverse pleasure out of putting X's next to the wrong answers, and when she put F's at the top of the papers, she always did it with a flair. She should have known better. She had Teddy's records and she knew more about him than she wanted to admit.

The records read:

> **1st Grade**: Teddy shows promise with his work and attitude, but poor home situation.

2nd Grade: Teddy could do better. Mother is seriously ill. He receives little help at home.

3rd Grade: Teddy is a good boy but too serious. He is a slow learner. His mother died this year.

4th Grade: Teddy is very slow, but well-behaved. His father shows no interest.

Christmas came, and the boys and girls in Miss Thompson's class brought her Christmas presents. They piled their presents on her desk and crowded around to watch her open them. Among the presents, there was one from Teddy Stallard. She was surprised that he had brought her a gift, but he had. Teddy's gift was wrapped in brown paper and was held together with scotch tape. On the paper were written the simple words: "For Miss Thompson. From Teddy." When she opened Teddy's present, out fell a gaudy rhinestone bracelet, with half the stones missing, and a bottle of cheap perfume.

The other boys and girls began to giggle and smirk over Teddy's gifts, but Miss Thompson at least had enough sense to silence them by immediately putting on the bracelet and putting some of the perfume on her wrist. Holding her wrist up for the other children to smell, she said, "Doesn't it smell lovely?" And the children, taking their cue from the teacher, readily agreed with "oohs" and "ahs."

At the end of the day, when school was over and the other children had left, Teddy lingered behind. He slowly came over to her desk and said softly, "Miss Thompson, you smell just like my mother, and her bracelet looks real pretty on you, too. I'm glad you liked my presents." When Teddy left, Miss Thompson got down on her knees and asked God to forgive her.

The next day when the children came to school, they were welcomed by a new teacher. Miss Thompson had become a different person. She was no longer just a teacher; she had become an agent of God. She was now a person committed to loving her children and doing things for them that would live on after her. She helped all the children, but especially the slow ones, and especially Teddy Stallard. By the end of that school year, Teddy showed dramatic improvement. He had caught up with most of the students and was even ahead of some.

Miss Thompson didn't hear from Teddy for a long time. Then, one day, out of the blue, she received a note that read:

Dear Miss Thompson:

I wanted you to be the first to know. I will be graduating first in my high school class.

Love,
Teddy Stallard

Four years later, another note came:

> Dear Miss Thompson:
>
> They just told me that I will be graduating first in my class. I wanted you to be the first to know. The university has not been easy, but I liked it.
>
> Love,
> Teddy Stallard

And four years later:

> Dear Miss Thompson:
>
> As of today, I am Theodore Stallard, M.D. How about that? I wanted you to be the first to know. I am getting married next month, the 27th to be exact. I want you to come and sit where my mother would sit if she were alive. You are the only family I have now. Dad died last year.
>
> Love,
> Teddy Stallard

Miss Thompson went to that wedding and sat where Teddy's mother would have sat. She deserved to sit there. She had done something for Teddy that he could never forget.

What can you give as a gift? Risk giving something that will live on after you. Be really generous. Give yourself.

One of Joan's Favorite Stories

INTEGRITY

"The Lord demands fairness in every business
deal. He established this principle."

PROVERBS 16:11

THE PREMIER DIFFERENCE

2010 National Rally

The most precious resource we have in America is the talent, resourcefulness and perseverance of the American people. President Bush said one time, "Government does not create wealth." American businesses, workers, farmers and entrepreneurs created the wealth of this country. There is no limit to what we can do when people have the freedom to make a better life for themselves.

Entrepreneurs create earning opportunities, and there is not a better example of that than a direct-selling company. The business model of direct sales companies is a superior model. Major skill is not required. Just a few basics are needed as you begin sharing the opportunity with others, and before you know it, one person's opportunity expands to hundreds more, either directly or indirectly.

Our type of business is called by many names—direct selling, network marketing, referral marketing or multilevel marketing. We in Premier like to call it direct servicing! Whatever you call it, you are in the best possible type of business. Having said that, what should our mark in the business world show others? What should be different about us? I believe there is one ingredient, and that is integrity. We should be people of integrity.

Our founding Scripture verse by which we operate our business in Premier Designs is Proverbs 16:11, "The Lord demands fairness in every business deal. He established this principle." Another version puts it this way, "[God] sets the standards for fairness." Our purpose in Premier is, first and foremost, to be ethical. To be ethical is to be honest and fair in our practices. Honesty is absolutely essential. Over and over in the book of Proverbs we are reminded that what ultimately matters to God is the quality of our character. His character sets the standard for us. I believe that the best way we can please God is to have integrity in all our business dealings. That is the Premier difference.

National Rally, 2010

Choose Wisely

Life is about choices—yours and mine.
I hope we make our choices good ones.

C Commitment to our Lord
and to excellence

H Hope and Home Shows

O Opportunity

I Integrity

C Compassion and Caring

E Experience—the best teacher

S Service, Servant, and
Spirit of Premier

Living with Integrity

A few years ago, a researcher at Santa Clara University in Silicon Valley, California, conducted a study of 1,500 business managers that revealed what workers value most in a boss. Employees said that they respect a leader who shows competence, who has the ability to inspire them, and who is skillful in providing direction.

But there was a fourth quality that they admired most in their leaders: integrity. Above all else, workers wanted a manager whose word is good, who is honest, and who can be trusted.

Integrity should characterize all Christian believers, no matter what their positions might be. According to Psalm 15, integrity is at the heart of every word and deed of a godly person. God always keeps His word, so if you are to be a godly person, you should do what you say you will do. Let's look more closely at the description of a person of integrity from Psalm 15:1-5.

- Leads a blameless life. (*That's certainly not possible on our own is it? It's something we choose, moment by moment, with the help of the Lord.*)

- Does what is right. (*Our Premier slogan, WIR—What Is Right, is in the Bible!*)

- Speaks the truth from a sincere heart. (*It always starts with our hearts, doesn't it?*)

❀ Refuses to slander others or speak evil of their friends. (*Not only that, but replaces unkind words with kind ones.*)

❀ Honors faithful followers of the Lord.

❀ Keeps promises even when it hurts. (*Never make a promise you cannot keep, and keep the promises you make. This is not always easy to do, but is essential if we are to live with integrity.*)

❀ Does not charge interest on money they lend. (*We should use our money to help others, not to profit on their misfortunes.*)

❀ Refuses to accept bribes.

Wow. That's quite a description. Do you know a person like that? If so, maybe you think, *Well, it's easy for her to be a good Christian. She doesn't have the same struggles I have. Of course she can live that way.* The truth is that living a life of integrity is a constant choice for all Christians. It's a moment-to-moment decision to live under the control of the Holy Spirit. It's not easy to walk blamelessly, but David has a wonderful promise for those who do. In closing this psalm, he says that the people who live this way will stand firm forever. They will never be shaken.

Home Office Managers Meeting, approximately 1995

Helpful Habits

Having a plan for our day helps us remain conscious of our priorities. Here are some things to include in your daily plan.

❀ Count your blessings.

❀ Remember that there is not another person like you. You are special.

❀ Do all things with love. Love yourself and love others.

❀ Pray for the day's activities and the people you will interact with.

Make these four things a habit in your life. My friend Mary Crowley always used to say, "In the beginning, we make our own habits, but in the end, our habits make us."

ETHICS CHECK

*O*ur company places ethics and morals at the top of our list of business standards. Integrity is very, very important in Premier. Our 2007 Verse of the Year says, "I know, my God, that you examine our hearts and rejoice when You find integrity there" (1 Chronicles 29:17). Isn't that awesome? God rejoices in this, so we know how important it is to Him. Our Purpose and our Philosophy is to honor God, serve people and enrich the lives of all we contact. And God examines our hearts and is pleased when He finds integrity there.

Where do ethics, honesty and integrity come from? Well, I submit to you it begins in childhood. Proverbs 22:6 says, "Train up a child in the way he should go." Are you teaching your children how to have integrity—to tell the truth? Did anyone teach you as a child to be honest? How? Think about it. I don't remember the positive side of my training as a child, but I vividly recall being punished for telling lies. The best way for us to teach integrity is to model it, day in and day out. Be consistent.

In order for Premier as a corporation to have integrity, those in management positions must model honesty and moral ethics in their own lives. Tom Watson has sometimes been referred to as the greatest golfer in the world. He has won nearly every major golf tournament at least once. He is known as a skilled golfer, but even more important, I think, is the fact that his integrity was evident at an early age.

In the first state tournament he ever entered, he put his putter down behind the ball on one of the greens. To his surprise, the

ball moved slightly. No one saw it, he was certain of that, but he knew the ball moved. He really wanted to win this tourney, but he also knew, without any hesitation, what he must do. He went to an official

2007 National Rally

and told him, "My ball moved." His admission cost him a stroke and he lost the hole. Tom had placed his personal integrity ahead of his keen desire to win. Happily, as it turned out, he did win the match, but he also lives with a clear, unblemished conscience. He modeled his convictions, and that's what we must do at Premier.

You may say, "Well, let Premier management believe how they want. I'm in my own business and I can do as I please." Is that true? No, I don't think so. You see, you represent Premier, and you may be the only part of Premier your neighbor sees. Your personal integrity is on the line, but because you are a representative of Premier, the company's integrity is also on the line.

I think most people basically know right from wrong, but let's do a quick "ethics check." Here are three questions to ask before you act.

❦ **IS IT LEGAL?** I am not only speaking of breaking society's law, but also of breaking a company policy of some kind. Remind yourself of our slogan: "WIR, WBP"—to do first what is right, and then what is best for Premier.

❦ **IS IT BALANCED AND FAIR?** Our Founding Verse is Proverbs 16:11, "The Lord demands fairness in every business deal." Am I following that guideline?

❦ **WILL IT MAKE ME FEEL GOOD ABOUT MYSELF?** How would I feel if it was published on the front page of the daily news? Would I like my immediate family to know?

There is no right way to do a wrong thing. Thinking about these questions can help keep us on that road of ethical integrity.

National Rally, 2007

THE JOB SECURITY STORY

A young man rushed into a gas station to use the pay phone. The gas station manager overheard the telephone conversation as the young man asked, "Sir, could you use a hardworking, honest young man to work for you?" Pause. "Oh, you already have a hardworking, honest young man? Okay. Well, thanks anyway."

The boy hung up the phone with a smile. Obviously happy, he was humming as he walked away. The gas station manager didn't understand. He asked, "How can you be so cheery? It sounded like the man you talked to already had someone and didn't want to hire you."

The young man answered, "Well, you see, I am the young man who works for him. I was just checking up on my job."

If you called your upline or your downline, could the same be said of you?

One of Joan's Favorite Stories

YOU ARE PREMIER

*B*ecause of our tremendous growth, it is more important than ever for people to understand who we are. You are Premier. We are Premier. We are all Premier! It is important that we never forget our Philosophy, Purpose and Plan.

Yes, we need good product and programs. But most of all we need people like you who care, and who want to share hope where it is needed. We are a people-driven company. Our people are Premier. We represent Premier wherever we are. I love it when my jewelry is recognized as Premier in some faraway city, but that gives me more responsibility as I represent Premier. "Will I impact people in a positive way? Will I be an influence for good?" If we are Premier, then what we say, how we look, and what we do all directly relate to our position as representatives of Premier Designs.

First, let's look at what we say. Honesty is more than telling the truth. It is a standard which governs our conduct, both in our personal and in our business lives. Lying and cheating is not being truthful. There are so many ways of being dishonest. For example, paying for a kit for someone, so you can win a sponsoring contest or become a Designer. Not only is that unhealthy and a poor business habit, it is cheating and dishonest.

Gossip is ugly, isn't it? Please don't participate in gossip. Don't pass on rumors. Rumors can be deadly. Why do we gossip? Some psychologists say that it is because of our desire to be "in the know" in order to exalt one's self-importance. Not good! We seem to be able to tame everything but our tongues. If it is not kind and helpful and true, then do not say it. Ask yourself, "Am I a part of the solution or am I adding to the problem?" If you are not helping, then keep quiet.

A life that is worthy of imitation is also one that is trustworthy. Let's make our word mean something. You are Premier!

Now let's look at another way we represent Premier. How do you make a statement without saying a word? Yes, it's your personal appearance! Our dress makes a statement. Many times, we dress to call attention to ourselves. What is the impression we are making? What are we saying about Premier? My friend Mary Crowley always told us that from the head up, we tell the world what we think of ourselves (and we spend hours in preparation). From the head down, the world will decide what they think of us! We dress to advertise our jewelry and, of course, we always wear Premier jewelry. We are in the fashion business and we count on you as representatives of Premier to lead by example.

Finally, what we do speaks volumes, and nothing feels better than doing what you know is right. The question is not *who* is right, but *what* is right? Our slogan for years has been WIR WBP—"What is right" and "What is best for Premier." The buck stops with Andy and me. We set the tone. We motivate by example. If we're not careful how we act—if we forget for one minute that we are Premier—then we can't expect you to follow in an acceptable manner. We must be wise in what we say, how we dress and the image we project. Example is a powerful teacher. I am Premier. You are Premier. We are all Premier!

National Rally, 2007

Good As Gold

I believe that the future of Premier Designs is in God's hands, but we are God's human instruments. We must tell the truth and keep our promises.

> If your word is good as gold,
> And your actions prove it true,
> Others hearing what you say
> Know they can depend on you.

Can your downline depend on you? Your upline? The Home Office? Is your word as good as gold?

A WOMAN OF YOUR WORD

God always keeps His word. In the book of Exodus, the Lord told the Israelites that He would free them from long slavery to the Egyptians. The awful plagues occurred against the Egyptians, then the angel of death passed over, and then their final deliverance came as they walked through the Red Sea. God kept His Word. It was just as He said.

In Matthew 28, we read the story of Jesus' resurrection and the empty tomb. An angel said to the women who had come to look at the tomb, "Do not be afraid, for I know you are looking for Jesus, who was crucified. He is not here—He has risen just as He said." God kept His word and He always will.

As I contemplated these two Biblical accounts, I was really encouraged in my spirit that God keeps His Word. But I also was reminded that I maybe have not always kept my word. God's Word is absolute Truth; are my words true, Lord?

Our words can be lots of things: sweet as honey, crude, gracious, encouraging, lying, discouraging. But can it be said our word is always true? No, I doubt it can. We are living in a time when truth seems to be nearly forgotten, and lies are easily and freely told in our families, as well as in high places of our government.

Sadly, sometimes we don't seem to take our words seriously

when we speak. The Bible has much to say about our words. In Matthew 12:34 we read, "Out of the abundance of the heart the mouth speaks." That means whatever is in your heart determines what you say. It goes on to say, "Every idle word men may speak, they will give account of it in the day of judgment" (Matthew 12:36). I often say, "What is in the well of your heart comes up and goes out in the bucket of speech."

Many things influence the things we say and how we say them. Proverbs 4:23 says, "Above all else, guard your heart, for everything you do flows from it," underscoring the influence our hearts and emotions have on us. If we want to be women of our word, we must guard our hearts, because they affect and determine what we say. And our words can determine how we influence others—for good or for ill.

I believe that the one woman who has most influenced the world was probably Mary, the mother of Jesus. She was chosen by God to bear the Son of God, to rock Him as a baby. She was chosen to nurture and train Him. Then she was chosen to give Him up to die for the whole world. Mary is a role model for any of us who desire to be an influence for God. How? She received a direct word from God and she believed it.

An angel told her she would conceive and give birth to a son, and call him Jesus. "How will this be," Mary asked the angel, "since

I am a virgin?" The angel explained that it would be through the Holy Spirit of God. And Mary's response to this incredible message? "I am the Lord's servant," Mary answered. "May it be to me according to your word."

Do you want to be a woman of influence where God has placed you? We don't have an angel speaking to us, but we can still humbly believe when He speaks through His Word—the Bible. God has chosen you to meet needs right where He has put you. To be women of our word involves integrity; that is the upside of keeping our word. God rejoices when He finds integrity in our hearts. Are we women of our word?

Word of Life Bible Conference, 2009

Do Your Best

The Lord does not expect us all to be famous, brilliant, beautiful or rich. But the Lord does require from us our very best. I have this little verse written in my Bible.

> You ask me what is the will of God,
> And I will answer true.
> It is the nearest thing that should be done
> That God can do through you!

THE ABCs OF PROVERBS

The Bible contains many types of writing. There is not a book in the Bible that is more down-to-earth and practical than the book of Proverbs. It's wisdom literature that instructs both young and old. It deals with common sense and good manners. It tells what the wise person would do in everyday situations, in finances, in work, and in family life. Proverbs is full of positive statements that tell us how to live successfully.

I found a little book years ago called *The ABCs of Proverbs*. I'm sorry that I don't know the author's name to give proper credit, but I'd like to share these ABCs with you. They're great.

A   Avoid all perverse talk, stay away from corrupt speech. Look straight ahead and fix your eyes on what lies before you. Mark out a straight path for your feet, and then stick to the path and stay safe. (*Proverbs* 4:24-26)

B   Be generous and you will be prosperous. Help others and they will help you. (*Proverbs* 11:25)

C   Correction and discipline are good for children. (*Proverbs* 29:15)

D   Don't make friends with people who have hot violent tempers. You might learn their habits and not be able to change. (*Proverbs* 22:24-25)

E   Enthusiasm without knowledge is not good: impatience will get you into trouble. (*Proverbs* 19:2)

F   Friends always show their love. What are brothers for if not to share trouble? (*Proverbs* 17:17)

G   God keeps every promise He makes. He is like a shield for all who seek His protection. (*Proverbs* 30:5)

H   Hot tempers cause arguments, but patience brings peace. (*Proverbs* 15:18)

I   If you refuse to learn, you are hurting yourself. If you accept correction, you will become wiser. (*Proverbs* 15:32)

J   What a Joy it is to find just the right word for the right occasion! (*Proverbs* 15:23)

K   Kind words bring life, but cruel words crush a man's spirit. (*Proverbs* 15:4)

L   Let other people praise you, even strangers—never do it yourself. (*Proverbs* 27:2)

M   Men may make their plans, but God has the last word. (*Proverbs* 16:1)

N   Never say something that isn't true. Have nothing to do with lies and misleading words. (*Proverbs* 4:24)

O   Old men are proud of their grandchildren, just as boys are proud of their fathers. (*Proverbs* 17:6)

P   Pay attention to your teacher and learn all you can. (*Proverbs* 23:12)

Q   Quote from King Solomon: Being wise is better than being strong. (*Proverbs* 24:5)

R   Refuse good advice and you are asking for trouble. Follow it and you are safe. (*Proverbs* 13:13)

S   Sometimes it takes a painful experience to make us change our ways. (*Proverbs* 20:30)

T   Too much honey is bad for you, and so is trying to win too much praise. (*Proverbs* 25:27)

U   Unreliable messengers cause trouble, but those who can be trusted make peace. (*Proverbs* 13:17)

V   Virtue is ignoring it when someone wrongs you. (*Proverbs* 19:11)

W   When you please the Lord, you can make enemies into friends. (*Proverbs* 16:7)

X   marks the spot next to the Proverb you need to work on.

Y   You do yourself a favor when you are kind; if you are cruel you only hurt yourself. (*Proverbs* 11:17)

Z   Zero in on the advice of King Solomon. (*Proverbs* 3:1, 3-4)

Senior Leadership Meeting, approximately 2001

The White Lie Cake Story

Alice was supposed to bake a cake for the church women's group bake sale, but forgot to do it until the last minute. She rummaged through her kitchen cabinets, found an angel food cake mix, and quickly made it, while she was drying her hair, dressing, and helping her son pack for Scout camp.

When Alice took the cake from the oven, the center had dropped flat and the cake was horribly disfigured. She said, "Oh, dear, there is not time to bake another one." This cake was important to Alice, because she did so want to fit in at her new church, and in her new community of friends. So, being inventive, she looked around the house for something to build up the center of the cake.

Alice found it in the bathroom—a roll of toilet paper. She plunked it in and then covered it with icing. Not only did the finished product look beautiful, it was shaped perfectly! Before she left the house, Alice woke her daughter Amanda and gave her specific instructions to be at the bake sale the moment it opened at 9:30 to buy that cake and bring it home.

When Amanda arrived at the church bake sale, she found that the cake had already been sold. Amanda grabbed her cell phone and called her mom. Alice was horrified! Everyone would find out, and then what would they think of her? She would be ostracized and ridiculed!

The next day, Alice promised herself she would try not to think about the cake. She decided to go to a fancy bridal shower luncheon at the home of a fellow church member and try to have a good time. She was hesitant to attend because the hostess was rather snobby and had looked down her nose at Alice, who was a single parent and not from the founding families of the city. But she forced herself to go anyway.

The meal was elegant, the company was definitely upper crust old South . . . and to Alice's horror, the CAKE in question was presented for dessert! Alice felt the blood drain from her body when she saw it. She started out of her chair to tell the hostess all about it, but before she could get to her feet, the Mayor's wife said, "What a beautiful cake!"

Alice, still stunned, sat back in her chair when she heard the hostess, a prominent church member say, "Thank you. I baked it myself."

Alice smiled and thought to herself, "God is so good."

One of Joan's Favorite Stories

Leadership

"Jesus said, 'Whoever wants to become great among you must be your servant, and whoever wants to be first must be slave of all.'"

MARK 10:42-44

BASICS OF LEADERSHIP

*C*onsider any true American leader, from Thomas Jefferson to Henry Ford to Martin Luther King, Jr. Each one was a dreamer, yet practical. Each one had dedication. Each one made a great impact. Jefferson gave us our Declaration of Independence; Ford, a vehicle that made us independent; and King, a dream of equal rights for all. The basic ingredients of leadership are integrity, dedication, humility, openness and creativity, plus that ability to dream great dreams—to have vision.

1. **INTEGRITY:** This includes honesty. But it's more than just telling the truth; it's a standard of moral honesty which governs and leads to our conduct. Aristotle wrote in his book *Ethics*, "If you would understand virtue, observe the conduct of virtuous men." And virtuous women, too, I might add.

Integrity begins at home. We must be careful how we live. The dozens of scandals these past few years in our nation are just the sum total of millions of undiscovered, uncounted small cheatings, evasions, cover-ups, half truths—not only in our alleged leaders, but in the whole of society.

2. **DEDICATION:** This is nothing more than a passionate belief in something. We must believe in Premier Designs and in our

Purpose, Philosophy and Plan. There's no stopping a leader when they are dedicated. Commitment is the basis for great works of art, inventions, scientific discoveries, etc. And it is what makes marriages, corporations and governments work.

3. HUMILITY: This involves a good self image. If you know who you are and have a healthy ego (which is okay), humility will follow. It means you can accept compliments graciously and take intelligent criticism without pouting or reacting. You are generous in forgiving.

4. OPENNESS: This is a willingness to try new things and hear new ideas. Being tolerant of views opposite to ours.

5. CREATIVITY: We are all born with some of this, but it gets lost or squashed along the way. We must restore our sense of wonder and awe, not only in the natural world around us, but in the business environment. Look at things with fresh new eyes. Leaders must encourage this kind of wonder and surround themselves with people who can look at things creatively.

I'll never forget the words of the cartoon character Pogo: "We have met the enemy, and he is us." If we don't have worthy leaders, it is our own fault. Our example is the Lord Jesus Himself. It is He who has taught us how to act. Did the Lord have integrity? Was He committed to the task? He was certainly humility personified, wasn't He? We know He was creative, just by the parables He used to teach. So He is truly our example, our leader in how we are to live.

National Rally Designer Meeting, 2005

No Limits

My dear friend Mary Crowley used to say, "I advance in God's potential, not limited by my own." That was her theme in life, and it can be ours as well! I would love to see every one of you so convinced of God's potential in and through you that you never, ever say, "I can't do that."

ENCOURAGE THE TIMID

*M*any of you do not relate to timidity or shyness. You are just the opposite! But there are many of you who have to work diligently to get out of your comfort zone of timidity. The apostle Paul recognized that timid people are special and are worthy of encouragement. "Brothers and sisters . . . encourage those who are timid. Take tender care of those who are weak. Be patient with everyone" (1 Thessalonians 5:14). If you lack confidence in this business, remember that our work is not who we are; it is only what we do! There's a difference between the two. Romans 12:3 says, "Do not think of yourself more highly than you ought." But that doesn't give you permission to think of yourself too lowly either, does it? We are all God's workmanship created in His image!

You may hear someone say, "Well, I am just a new Jeweler. I could never stand up at training. I don't have the confidence to do it by myself." You can and should help her gain confidence. "Encourage those who are timid." A new Jeweler needs help easing into her new role.

After you sponsor Amy Timid, you will do her Training Show. Give her a non-threatening role—perhaps getting the models dressed with jewelry, or holding the chart showing the Hostess Plan. Have her sit with you at check-out, if possible. Then, commit to be with her at two more of her Home Shows, where you will share in the presentation. If she asks you to attend more than the two shows, please encourage her one more time! After that, she can do it all herself.

Please don't assume Amy Timid is not really timid, or that it is no big deal! It is a big deal, and she does need encouragement. It won't be forever, but be willing to give her a good start. You are responsible for Amy Timid, and Premier expects your best effort.

Along with encouraging, we need to "take tender care of those who are weak." Sometimes we demand more than someone can personally give. We have to admit that we sometimes expect some young Jewelers to do what they just can't do. Be gentle and helpful and pass on some hope. At times we also are placed in difficult situations, and maybe feel discouraged and fearful. I've been there. Many people have come my way through the years to care for and encourage me.

Next, we are to "be patient with everyone." Everyone? Yes! God promises, "My grace is sufficient for you, for My power is made perfect in weakness" (2 Corinthians 12:9). God's grace is our ultimate encouragement. So take care of and encourage your sisters in your upline and downline. We all need it!

Roundup, 2010

Time for Everything

Time is a precious commodity, isn't it? We often say, "I just don't know where the time went!" Or, "I am sorry I'm late. Time just got away from me." Each of us is allotted a total of 168 hours per week, no more and no less than anyone else. God, our Creator, is in charge of time, and the Bible says, "There is a time for everything" (Ecclesiastes 3:11).

We are responsible for our time. We use it, save it, spend it, waste it, lose it. But how do we guard it? Are we careful stewards of what God has entrusted to us? Time seems like such a small thing, and yet, we reveal so much by what we do with it.

LEADING IS SERVING

*D*id you know that the King James Bible uses the term *leader* only six times? More frequently, the role is called *servant*. Moses, as great a leader as he was, was not called "Moses, my leader," but "Moses, my servant." And this is exactly what Christ taught. Jesus said in Mark 10:43-45, "Whoever wants to become great among you must be your servant, and whoever wants to be first must be slave of all. For even the Son of Man did not come to be served, but to serve, and to give His life as a ransom for many."

The term *servant* implies low respect and low honor. Most people are not attracted to such a low-value role. However, when Jesus used the term, it was a synonym for greatness, and that was a revolutionary idea. The Lord Jesus defined leadership as service. A true leader is concerned primarily with the welfare of others. And, because their welfare is paramount, the leader's responsibility is to train others to also become servants, remembering that everything we do must be done to glorify the Lord, not for our personal gain.

Our role as a servant is to be one filled with happiness and joy. That is the spirit of service. Not doing it because we have to, but joyfully, motivated by love. Love is not choosy; it's all-inclusive.

Jesus said we are to love even our enemies. Love is active, not passive. Our reminder of that is in 1 John 3:18: "Dear children, let us stop just saying we love each other, let us really show it by our actions."

2001 National Rally

We say, "Let me know if I can do anything to help." Love says, "I'm fixing dinner for your family tomorrow night. What time can I deliver it?" You have a new Jeweler who is unable to attend an important training. We say, "I'll send you the notes." Love says, "I would be happy to go over the material with you. May I come tomorrow night?"

Paul said in Galatians 5:13, "Serve one another in love." True greatness is found in giving of yourself in service to others, not in coaxing or inducing others to serve you. The true leader is focused on the service he or she can give to God and to others.

Designer Leadership Conference, 2001

THE CHOICE IS YOURS

We recently visited the city of Prague in the Czech Republic. It is said to be one of the most beautiful cities in the world, and I agree with that assessment. It's filled with countless beautiful castles, churches and museums—many of which took over 500 years to build.

That is so difficult for us to imagine, not seeing the completion of our work in our own lifetimes. America is the land of the "instant" everything. That's not what we found in Europe, and it's not what we read in the Bible either, is it? In Deuteronomy 6 we read, "You shall love the Lord your God with all your heart and with all your soul and with all your might. These words, which I am commanding you today, shall be on your heart. You shall teach them diligently to your sons and shall talk of them when you sit in your house and when you walk by the way and when you lie down and when you rise up." Each generation is responsible to and for its successors. Each Designer here is responsible to her downline. And each of you is responsible for your successor. Ever thought about that?

The poet Longfellow said, "We judge ourselves by what we feel we are capable of doing. Others judge us by what we have already done." I believe he was correct. You who have built your businesses are leading the way for those who follow. You are responsible for being that mature example, not really caring who receives the credit for a job well done.

2008 National Rally

As I looked at that beautiful city of Prague—the city of 1,000 spires and 700 clocks—I was thankful that those builders of so long ago, who worked over the course of five centuries, didn't quit. They were building for the future of their families and others who followed them. They fulfilled their responsibilities, and because of them, we could stand and enjoy that beautiful city of Prague. They made good choices.

The decisions and choices that we make will affect many others for months and years ahead. Each Designer here is accountable for preserving and passing on the Premier story. You are responsible for upholding the Philosophy and the Purpose of Premier. To make sure that we make wise choices, it's helpful if we stay focused. I am suggesting that you keep your focus on keeping your downline strong with new growth. Your example and your practice will ensure that Premier's second generation will also be strong and active, and a blessing to those who join us.

Richard DeVos, the co-founder of the Amway Corporation and an active member of the Direct Selling Association for many years, has outlined four stages in the lifetime of a business.

1. THE CREATIVE STAGE: There are many words we could use to describe this first stage. Just think back to your beginning days as a new Jeweler. You are excited, hopeful, enthusiastic, fearful, confident, proud, eager to learn everything. Nothing can stop you! You begin to set goals, your creative juices are flowing, and you have HOPE.

2. THE MANAGEMENT STAGE: The second stage may begin at any time. In Premier, that would be the Designer level. Slowly, but very surely, we see Designers reach a "comfort zone." You say, "I've made it! I have arrived! I must take a rest and celebrate." That early enthusiasm is slowly diminishing. Time is now spent in the office and on the computer, more than with the people. And who has time to do Home Shows? This is time to take your pulse—your Premier pulse. Is it still beating for Premier? If not, you may soon move into Stage Three.

3. THE DEFENSIVE STAGE: This is a time when we see nothing wrong with our lack of personal growth. We rationalize, "After all, I am a Designer now. I may have lost two personal first-levels, but I can replace them soon—no problem." When you begin to defend your actions like this, watch out! That exciting Stage One is a long way back. Bankruptcy, also known as the Blaming Stage, might soon rear its ugly head.

4. **THE BLAMING STAGE:** You blame the company for your business downturn. You blame the economy for the lack of opportunities. You might blame your family for keeping you too busy.

As Queen Mother, I would love to just command with my magic wand and you would all be Seven Diamonds with the enthusiastic excitement of a brand-new Designer! I would love to do that, but I can't. I'm sure Andy would fix it if he could, but he can't make that choice for you either. You must make your own choice! Taking responsibility for our own activities is one of the marks of maturity. We as leadership in Premier must accept that responsibility.

One of our most successful field leaders has said for many years, "Make it a serious goal to become a Designer every year." That is good advice, believe me. Every year try to recover some of that Stage One creativity and enthusiasm. Be a leader! Don't be "defensive." Be a leader! Don't "blame." Be a leader! If you get tired—and you will—you may have to rest for a moment. But don't give up!

We owe it to those who built Premier in the early days. We

owe it to those who are coming to help us in this present time, and we owe it to those who will join Premier in the future, in order to preserve Premier for the second and third generations. I believe we are accountable to God, who has raised up this company called Premier to serve Him and to enrich the lives of all we meet.

National Rally Designer Dinner, 2008

Stuck in the Doldrums

Sometimes it's hard to know what to say to others who are struggling and may be stuck. The "Feel, Felt, Found" formula is a proven way to listen with understanding and to encourage someone to take the next step.

> "I can see how you feel."
>
> "I once felt that way."
>
> "I found that by doing this and this and this, I would overcome."

Try it and see if you can help someone out of their personal or business doldrums.

OPERATION PREMIER

*Y*ears ago Andy and I became friends with John and Joann Corts who worked with Billy Graham Crusades. John wrote a plan for that organization called "Operation Andrew" to help people work together as a team. I adapted his plan and renamed it "Operation Premier." We are a team at Premier and we want to function as a unified team.

There are five steps to Operation Premier. These steps will help you build your business, enhance your relationships, and I think they will be useful in strengthening your commitment to God and to Premier. The key word is LOOK.

1. **LOOK UP:** We can't have good relationships and build our Premier family without God's help. We must look up for wisdom as we deal with our downlines, our uplines, our sisters and cousins in Premier. Charlie Brown was pleading one time with Lucy to be tolerant and understanding. He said, "Lucy, you must be loving. The world really needs to be loved." Lucy screamed back, "Look, Blockhead, the world I love. It's the people I can't stand." We've all felt like that at times, but if we get in the habit of looking up, we have a Helper. Look up and pray for help. Look up and pray for wisdom. God is faithful. He is big enough for any need we have.

2. **LOOK AROUND:** In God's providence, He has placed you near

all the people in your life and in your Premier business. Look around and be alert to needs. Recognize that every Jeweler has strengths and weaknesses. We all have needs for security and recognition and belonging. We all have responsibilities other than Premier. Other Jewelers are just like you. That ought to change our perspective, right? Look around and see things from another person's perspective—your Hostesses, your Jewelers, your friends, your family. It will make a difference.

3. LOOK OUT: This doesn't mean to beware of or watch out for; rather, it means to be on the lookout for ways to build up relationships. Be on the lookout for ways to encourage and to minister. Our express purpose in Premier is to serve others and to enrich lives. Maybe someone needs a hug or a smile. Maybe they need help with booking or Hostess coaching. Are you willing to be on the lookout for those needs?

4. LOOK AFTER: Stay close to those whom God has entrusted to your care. I really believe that He has placed certain people in your Premier family for a purpose. After you have looked up and prayed for them faithfully, and after you have looked around and looked out for needs, then you can look after them. You can be available with practical help and concern. Are you willing to expend the energy and time that is necessary to look after your relationships?

5. **LOOK FORWARD:** Look to the future. Set goals. Write them down and tell someone what they are. Make a commitment. Someone has said that our business is like riding a bicycle— either you keep moving or you fall down. Be faithful to that which God has given you and always look forward with hope. The future is as bright as the promises of God. The Bible says, "The eyes of the Lord range throughout the earth to strengthen those whose hearts are fully committed to Him" (2 Chronicles 16:9). What a great truth. Our heavenly Father is looking out for us. His watchful care for us is constant.

So keep looking up, around, out, after and forward. Doing these things will not only build up your team, but it will also build up your life.

Roundup, 1995

Spelling Leadership

Jim Miller, of Miller Business Systems, provided the following acrostic on leadership in his book, *The Corporate Coach*. I have "Hornerized" it a bit.

L   Listen with an open mind.

E   Enable others to do their best.

A   Have Ambition, team goals and a vision.

D   Work with Desire and enthusiasm.

E   Be an Example and role model.

R   Respect others and their abilities.

S   Have Self-esteem, poise, confidence.

H   Have Heart; show concern and empathy.

I   Take Initiative to make things happen.

P   Have Patience; be quick to praise and slow to criticize.

OUR COMMITMENTS

2008 National Rally

We all have many commitments. What determines the commitments that you make? Our first commitment is to the Lord, according to Proverbs 16:3, "Commit to the Lord whatever you do, and He will establish your plans." I believe that God has ultimate control over all my activity, so I need to commit my work to Him first. I believe God has called me to do this work, and has not yet un-called me. So I will continue to commit it to Him.

Do you have a goal? If you do, you must have a commitment to that goal. I am a believer in doing things right—doing things the best we know how. I believe we should have a commitment to excellence! Whatever work you are doing today, commit to excellence when you work. Commit to excellence in your relationships. Commit to excellence with your Hostesses. Relationships must be kept fresh.

From the beginning God intended that we should work. Adam worked in the garden. Moses was a shepherd, as was David. Peter and Andrew were fishermen. From the earliest days in our country, the founding fathers had a desire to work hard. God ordained work from the beginning. So let us commit to our work.

Commit to your downline. Give your Jewelers your best so that they will have successful businesses. Be that good example they can follow. Do all you can for your downline in the beginning, and then show them how to row their own boats. After that, your commitment should be to continue alongside them, to be available when and if you are needed.

Commit also to our company, Premier Designs! Seek to abide by the rules and regulations, to be honest and fair in all your dealings, and to uphold the principles and values of Premier Designs. Make up your mind, and then follow through on your commitments.

National Rally, 2008

YOUR WORK

"All hard work brings a profit, but
mere talk leads only to poverty."

PROVERBS 14:23

Love Your Work

We believe that hard work, together with honesty, integrity and service, will build Premier to heights we dare to dream about. It is like a small little kernel of corn. What can be done with one kernel of corn? Certainly nothing if it lies dormant on the shelf. It might feed a baby chick for one meal. But let's work with this kernel. Let's plant it, water it, cultivate it. What would happen then? It would produce a corn stalk with at least one ear of corn that has many kernels.

Suppose we work hard and plant all those kernels next year? In the fall, we could harvest hundreds of ears of corn, with thousands and thousands of kernels. If these were planted again, our harvest would be tremendous! From this one original grain of corn would come millions of bushels. But not by being lazy. It comes from hard work! Do you see the possibilities? Why, the potential is unlimited!

Premier started in November 1985 with one kernel. Then there were two. After much hard work there were dozens, hundreds, and now there are thousands. But without the hard work, the kernels of corn would not grow. We are convinced that work is the necessary and key ingredient for growing.

Work for what you believe in. My precious friend Mary Crowley used to quote a little rhyme:

> If you work for the thing you believe in,
> You're rich though the way is rough.
> If you're working only for money,
> You can never earn quite enough.

She really believed this. She's a marvelous example of one who fell in love with hard work, with the enjoyment of it and the accomplishment of it. She often said, "Find something to do that you love so much, you will do it for free. Then learn to be so good at it that the world pays you well to do it." Hard work—Mary built a multi-million dollar company on this premise.

In Proverbs 14:23 we read, "Work brings profit; talk brings poverty." Work is something you do, not just talk about. Throughout history work has been man's chief activity, and the importance of labor is obvious in our country. Some people, unfortunately, have little respect for an honest day's work. I read about a sign at the entrance of a great manufacturing plant that reads, "If you are like a wheelbarrow, going no farther than you are pushed, you need not apply for work here." Some people need to be pushed in order to really accomplish something worthwhile. Is that you?

There are three kinds of people who work:

✤ Those who make things happen.

❦ Those who watch things happen.

❦ Those who have no idea what has happened!

Which category are you? Remember, work brings profit. The Bible says, "A person can do nothing better than to eat and drink and find satisfaction in their own toil" (Ecclesiastes 2:24). How many of us work hard and are really satisfied with our work? That's a worthy goal, isn't it?

National Rally, 1991

Just Five More Minutes

In Ted Engstrom's book, *Pursuit of Excellence*, he writes about why some people excel and others don't. His premise is "just five minutes more." One of his basic points is this: "Just five minutes more of asking God to give you the special guidance you so desperately need." Those five minutes can make all the difference. And God will give you that guidance. He promises, "I will guide you along the best pathway for your life [the very best one!]. I will advise you and watch over you" (Psalm 32:8).

KEEPING A HEALTHY BALANCE

We are living in a health-conscious society. Walking, jogging, aerobics, yoga, all kinds of workouts at the gym—these are all very popular today. Listen in on any conversation and if you wait long enough, it will turn to the subject of dieting, some new recipe, or the latest 10-minute exercise drill of some kind. Eating the right kind of food, getting exercise, and resting are generally accepted to be the basic ingredients of good health. Let's look at how this relates to keeping a healthy balance in our Premier business.

First, to stay healthy we need food, and our "food" comes from several sources. It could be our beautiful high fashion jewelry—the absolute best. That is great food! There are local trainings to attend. Our trainers are the best, with new and innovative ideas. There's also the National Rally once a year. What great food that is for our business! Do you ever think, *I don't need to really worry about attending Rally. I know how to do a Home Show.* You know what? Without the food of new training and new ideas, your business will grow weak and may starve to death.

Next, is exercise. Exercise is good for us physically and mentally, to keep us alert and energetic. Losing the habit of doing Home Shows is like not exercising. If you don't have at least one Home Show each month, you become sluggish in that area. You cannot keep your business on the cutting edge! Your Premier business health will suffer.

Another good exercise is sharing the Premier opportunity with someone else. You know, when you don't use muscles for a while, they become sluggish. It's the same with sharing. If we don't share about Premier for awhile, we become timid and sluggish in that area.

One more very important example of exercise is having a serving heart. The world is just crying out for service. You can buy jewelry at any number of stores, boutiques, or kiosks. But you cannot buy personal service and care. Let's be sure we use our service muscles!

The final ingredient for a healthy balance is rest. We can eat the correct food and faithfully exercise, but without rest we are not at our best. Rest is vital. Delegating work can keep others busy and can alleviate any stress you may be feeling. I have heard Andy say many times, "You have my permission to take the day off." When you are tired, take the time to rest. The Bible says, "Rest in the Lord, and wait patiently for Him" (Psalm 37:7). That is the ultimate rest. No phones, no email, no internet. Just quiet rest.

That one is easy to forget, because rest has not been sufficiently important to me. But if I am honest with myself, I must admit that to have a true and good balance in my life and in my business, I need all three: Food + Exercise + Rest = Perfect Balance.

National Rally, 2009

What Is Your Perspective?

A story is told about a man who came upon three laborers who were working on a large building under construction. The man asked each one, "What are you doing?" The first worker replied, "Stone cutting." The second laborer smiled and said, "Putting in my time until a better job comes along." The third man paused a moment, and then said simply, "I'm building a cathedral." Keep your eyes on the big picture.

ACHIEVING YOUR GOALS

Why is our work so frustrating to us? Why do we procrastinate doing something we say that we love? One reason is that we may have set no goals. We see our business as a hobby that can be picked up at will or stuffed in the closet to hide when it interferes with our short-term fun. A second reason is that if we do have goals, they may be completely unrealistic ones.

1995 National Rally

Here are some practical steps to setting realistic goals. In her book titled I Can; You Can, Too, author and speaker Mamie McCullough shares her Goals Achievement Formula:

1. Identify your goals.

2. List benefits you will receive from achieving your goals.

3. Set a deadline for achieving your goals.

4. Identify the major obstacles you will face.

5. Identify the skills or knowledge required to reach your goals.

6. Develop a specific plan of action.

Be specific and put each of the above steps in writing. We are told in Proverbs 16:3 to commit and entrust our work to the Lord and our plans will succeed. This verse doesn't say, "Plan, dream, desire, want, and then you'll have success." No, it says first commit to God whatever you do. I would like to challenge all of you to try harder to do those things you think about and dream about, but never get around to doing. Try setting your goals and then WORK, WORK, WORK. Your plans will succeed if you commit them to God, serve others, and enrich lives through your work.

National Rally, 1995

Four Loves

Mary Crowley used to say that when you are building your business, you need to look for people to sponsor who have four loves.

❧ Love of people

❧ Love to work

❧ Love to learn

❧ Love the product

You'll notice that the list doesn't say to look for a professional sales person, or someone who dresses like a fashion model, or one who can speak well in public. Those things can all be taught, if they love to learn and love to work. Above all they must have a love for people—people of all kinds and all sizes and shapes. That's the real key. They must love people.

A CLEAN SWEEP

$\mathcal{S}$ometimes we need a clean sweep in our business, just as we need in our closets at home. There's nothing I like better than to get into my closet and clean it out. I love organizing it to make it more user-friendly, instead of being a treasure hunt each time I go there!

I've heard it said that if you haven't worn something in the last two years, you don't need it. So that is my basic plan when I tackle my closet. I pull out the clothes I haven't worn lately. But then I see an outfit and think, "I might use it next month or next year. I love the color and the fabric. And those buttons are adorable. I really need to keep this." No! Back to the plan. Move it out. Let's face it, bad habits die hard. But what satisfaction I feel when I finish! And the closet will be much more useful and efficient after the purging.

It's the same with our businesses. We keep things around that only clutter it up or that continually drag us down. Maybe we have regrets: "If I had just done two more shows, I could have made the 25-Home Show Club." Please don't hang onto that. Move it out to make room for new opportunities that are coming this year. Maybe there are small failures: "I really let my Hostess down by not having enough sales to qualify as a Home Show."

Well, take that off the hanger and get rid of it. Replace it by learning how to better coach your Hostesses.

Our "closet" is looking a little better now, but there are still some things hidden over there in the corner—things we just don't want to deal with. We try to hide them, but they really need to go:

- hurts
- disappointments
- broken jewelry
- goals we didn't meet
- cancelled shows
- promises we didn't keep
- unhappy customers
- gossip
- unkind words
- stubborn attitudes
- dumb mistakes
- jealousy

You can make a long list of clutter and junk, can't you? So can I. Maybe we should adopt an old Italian custom I read about. On New Year's Eve in certain areas of Italy, the streets are cleared of all traffic and pedestrians. Then at the stroke of midnight, the windows of the houses fly open. To the sound of laughter, music and fireworks, families pitch out old crockery, broken ornaments, hated furniture, and personal possessions that remind them of something in the past year that they are determined to get rid of.

You alone are the one who can make a difference in your messy, cluttered closet. If your business isn't what you want it to be, then get busy and start pitching the junk. Make room for new goals and opportunities!

National Rally, 2000

Make Today Great

Success is like housework. You have to do it every day, again and again. This is true in every area of your life. Today is the first day of the rest of your life. Make it a good one. Today is the only day you have. Make it great.

Wisdom and Common Sense

*I*n 1 Kings 3:5, we read that the Lord appeared to King Solomon in a dream and told him to ask for anything he wanted, and it would be given to him. What would you ask for? Solomon asked to have wisdom and common sense. He responded, "Give me an understanding mind so that I can govern your people well and know the difference between right and wrong. For who by himself is able to carry such a heavy responsibility?" (1 Kings 3:9). God was pleased with his reply. He gave Solomon not only great wisdom, but also what he did not ask for—great riches and honor.

Wisdom is the ability to see life from God's perspective. It is the ability to use facts and knowledge to come to correct conclusions. Wisdom is having the insight plus the common sense to solve a problem. The following fable is an excellent illustration of the need for common sense.

Once there was a Tortoise who decided he wanted to possess all the wisdom in the whole world. Then all the kings and counselors would turn to him, the wisest of them all, whenever they needed to solve a problem.

He set out to collect all the wisdom in the world, and each time he gathered some, he put it into a gourd. When there was no more wisdom to be had and the gourd was stuffed full, he sealed it tightly with a roll of leaves. He decided to hide the gourd on top of a very high tree that no one else could climb. He tied a rope to the neck of the gourd, and then tied the two ends together. He put the rope loop over his head so the gourd was resting on his stomach, connected to his neck.

The Tortoise began to climb the tree. He would struggle up a ways, and then would slip all the way back to where he started. The gourd was in his way, but he didn't give up. He climbed and slipped, and climbed and slipped. After a while, he heard someone laughing. He turned around and saw a hunter watching him. "Friend," the hunter said, "Why don't you hang that gourd behind you if you want to climb that tree?"

Having all the wisdom in the world doesn't count for much without some good old-fashioned common sense.

National Rally, 1992

The Slim Margin of Success

At the end of the baseball season, do you know how many hits separate a .290 batter from someone who averages the coveted .300? It's not 100 or even 50 hits; it's only five. Five more hits over the six-month season—that's less than one more hit per month. But what a difference that one hit can make. For one thing, it makes a huge difference in their salary!

Success is often measured by slim margins—just one more run, one more strike. One more phone call to a Hostess. One more Home Show.

Consider the Ant

Proverbs 6:6-9 tells us to look at the ant and "consider its ways and be wise." So, what do ants teach us?

ANTS ARE ORGANIZED (Proverbs 6:7). They have no guide, overseer, or ruler, but they work together. The other day I watched three teeny, tiny ants try to move a twig. They tried every angle to get that twig moving, but couldn't do it. Soon, there came five or six more ants, and together they all carried that twig to the anthill. They live together, work together, and help each other achieve their goals.

ANTS PREPARE AHEAD OF TIME (Proverbs 6:8). They have foresight. They gather and store food in the summer, when it's abundant. That means they can have a good winter when food is harder to find, because they are prepared.

ANTS ARE NOT LAZY (Proverbs 6:6,9). Anthills are teeming with hard workers, always busy, busy, busy. They care for their queen, and continuously dig new tunnels to make room for new ants and food. A lazy ant wouldn't last long.

So learn from the ant, and don't be a lazybones!

National Rally, 1992

A BLUEPRINT FOR YOUR BUSINESS

*E*ver watched a house being built? What's the first thing that's needed? The blueprints. A plan. Then the foundation is poured and the shell of the house goes up. It gradually takes shape, and one day you have a beautiful home—because of wise planning.

2010 National Rally

Was it always easy? Perfect weather? Supplies and workers always on time? No way! Could the carpenter just put things up without measuring, or the electrician string wires any which way? No. Did one person do it all? Of course not.

It's the same with Premier. We had a plan—a blueprint of how to build a business that would Honor God and Serve Others. Part of that plan was to find the right people for the job. God has brought people with all different gifts and abilities together and is using them to build Premier Designs.

Have you drawn up your blueprints for your business? What are your goals? You need the right plan to build a successful business. Proverbs 24:3-4 says that any enterprise is:

1. Built by wise planning,
2. Becomes strong through common sense,
3. Profits wonderfully by keeping abreast of the facts.

These are the three phases of our business, and of yours. You are the Chairman of the Board, the Secretary and the Treasurer of your Premier business. You have complete control, and also complete responsibility. Can you do it alone? No. None of us can build a business alone. We need fellow Jewelers, our uplines and downlines, our Hostesses and our customers. We need just the right people to join our team.

So, we build a business with a good plan, and then it becomes strong through common sense! The common sense of having a budget. The common sense of paying our bills on time. The common sense of encouraging and appreciating our people. The common sense of self-discipline. That's not always easy, especially for certain sanguine personalities, but common sense tells us that we need discipline to work our business consistently.

The third phase—profit—comes from "keeping abreast of the facts," Proverbs says. This means working hard to learn all we can. It means knowing where we are in relation to our goals, and being the best we can be. And profit isn't just money. Fulfillment in enriching lives is great personal profit. Noticing what people need and showing you care. Seeing your people grow. These intangible rewards mean we are running a profitable business.

So build with a good plan. Become strong using common sense. Profit by keeping abreast of the facts. I believe that if you do this, you will have a successful Premier business.

National Rally, 1990

The Joy of Working

I hope we all know the joy of working. All of us heard this little prayer when we were growing up.

> Now I lay me down to sleep,
> I pray the Lord my soul to keep.
> If I should die before I wake,
> I pray the Lord my soul to take.

There is a lesser-known second verse, of which we all need to be reminded.

> Now I wake me up to work,
> I pray the Lord I will not shirk.
> If I should die before tonight,
> I pray the Lord my work's all right.

May God make our work "all right," to honor Him and be a blessing to others.

THE CHASING A DEAD DOG STORY

*J*read this story several years ago and I believe it's a dramatic illustration for us, both in our personal lives and with our business relationships.

A certain older dog had been left with a neighbor while its owner was away on vacation. The shock of being away from home proved to be too much for the old dog's constitution. The woman got up one morning and found him dead under her kitchen table.

In a big city, giving away a live dog is difficult enough, but whatever would she do with a canine carcass? After numerous phone calls and several futile attempts to dispose of it, her only recourse seemed to be the local humane society. They agreed to arrange a burial if she would bring the remains to their headquarters.

Since the woman had to go there by bus, transporting the body posed something of a problem. After considering the various alternatives, she decided to put the dead dog in an old suitcase and simply carry him to his final resting place, while still maintaining a maximum degree of dignity. She decided this would be the least obvious method, thereby decreasing attention upon her.

Halfway to her destination, she had to change buses, and a young man very graciously offered to carry her piece of luggage.

He murmured something about it being a dead weight, and when she refused to divulge the contents, he must have concluded that she was smuggling gold or silver. At any rate, she boarded the next bus, expecting the kind gentleman to follow. She looked back just in time to see the culprit absconding down a back alley with the suitcase. Her first impulse was to give chase; but then, she was struck by the absurdity of the situation. Chasing a dead dog—of all things!

How about you? Chasing any dead dogs in your business or relationships lately?

One of Joan's Favorite Stories

SERVING
WITH LOVE

"Serve one another humbly in love."

GALATIANS 5:13

Year of the Towel

One of my friends suggested that it might be a good idea if, like the Chinese, we gave names to our years. She said we should call 2010 "The Year of the Towel." We're living in a year when people are continually asking, "Who has the authority to do that? Who has the power?" Why don't we ask, "Where's the towel?"

My friend went on to explain that she was referring to the Gospel of John's account of the feast of Passover, when the Lord Jesus was having His last supper with His disciples. John wrote this: "[Jesus] got up from the table, took off His robe, wrapped a towel around His waist, and poured water into a basin. Then He began to wash the disciples' feet, drying them with the towel He had around Him . . . Jesus said, 'I have given you an example to follow. Do as I have done to you'" (John 13:4-5, 15).

What had He done? He had served. The One who had all power and all authority laid it down to serve. And in the future, the disciples no longer asked, "Where is my power?" They remembered what Jesus had shown them, and what Jesus had said, "Whoever wants to be great among you must be your servant" (Matthew 20:26). Their main concern, then, became to serve, and to encourage others to do the same.

The Year of the Towel. Wouldn't that be a good way to encourage us to think of how we can serve others, forgetting any sacrifice we are making? In these days of power-hungry leaders, we can paint a different picture—serve, serve, serve. Serving one another at home and in our family of Jewelers. Serving with care. Serving with love. We can all make a difference.

Regional Rally, 2010

Serving with Love

Serving others is not always easy to do, but it is a big part of Premier Designs. We are a "people" business, and to be successful, we must be able to serve with love. Some people are very hard to love. It does not always come naturally. But love never gives up. Love goes on forever. Love builds people up, and people build our business.

CUSTOMERS ARE NUMBER ONE

*O*ur customer is the most important person in our business. A customer is not dependent on us; we are dependent on her. Customers are not an inter-
ruption to our work; they are the purpose of it. A customer does us a favor when she contacts us; we are not doing her a favor by being of service.

2009 National Rally

A customer is part of our business, not an outsider. A cus-
tomer is not just money in our pocket. She is a human being with feelings, like our own. A customer is a person who comes to us with needs and wants. It is our job and privilege to help meet those needs and desires.

Customers deserve the most courteous attention we can give them. They are the lifeblood of our business. They pay our salaries. Without them, we would have no business. Don't ever forget it!

National Rally, 2009

REAL GIVING

*G*od's great gift to mankind was motivated by one thing—love. "God so loved the world that He gave His only Son," the Bible tells us. What about our giving? Is it motivated by love alone? And what do we have to give? I suggest five things: giving our time, ourselves, encouragement, compliments, and giving of our means. The person who exemplifies the Premier spirit is one who will give these things in love.

1. OUR TIME: This is one of the greatest gifts you can give anyone. We must be sensitive to the needs of those who need our time and attention. First, we need to give time to our husbands—time when we give them 100 percent of our attention. And it doesn't need to be a long time. It can be very precious when it's just two minutes of undivided attention.

Next, to our children. You're being pulled in four directions and then along comes your child pulling at the same time. It's tempting to say, "I don't have time right now." How much better to give your attention to them for just a few seconds, if that's all you have. Acknowledge them. Give of your time.

And to your Jewelers. When we give someone our time and attention, they know they are special.

2. OURSELVES (physically): This kind of giving involves your physical presence. What a gift it is, when you personally and physically show up to help, when you work alongside others, and when you pour your energy into the group.

3. ENCOURAGEMENT: Proverbs 12:25 says, "Anxious hearts are very heavy, but a word of encouragement does wonders." We all experience times of discouragement, and just the right words affect us profoundly. Words of encouragement and praise don't always come naturally, but we can all work on it. Fine tune that gift so you can give it more often. I guarantee you that a word of encouragement will brighten anyone's day. And the more difficult the person, the more they need encouragement.

4. COMPLIMENTS (kind words): Proverbs tells us, "A word fitly spoken is like apples of gold in pictures of silver" (Proverbs 25:11). That's what a compliment is—the truth, fitly spoken, in love and with kindness. A beautiful gift to give.

Have you ever received a compliment that didn't sound genuine, or felt like flattery rather than a true compliment? Perhaps that person was in search of a compliment herself. The difference between flattery and genuine, kind compliments is motivation. Is the compliment truly a gift I desire to give to that person, or is it a way to get something back for myself? It's the same with the tone of our words. Unkind words are not gifts we should give anyone, but kind words are a treasure.

5. OUR MEANS (money): What we do with our money is a very personal thing. Who we give it to is a matter between our heavenly Father and us. And I'm not talking about large sums of money. I'm talking about being on the lookout for small ways we can be of help to others financially. Maybe a few dollars would make the difference between a Jeweler going to Rally or not, or being able to renew her contract. Maybe you can pay for a babysitter for a single mom, so she can do that extra Home Show, or buy her a tank of gas. The value of the gift is not measured in dollars.

A small gift given in love—a little of our time, of ourselves, of encouragement, of kind words, of our means—will multiply and multiply and multiply.

For instance, a penny is the smallest coin we have. Most of us don't even pay attention to a penny here or a penny there. But, say I hire you to do a job. I offer you a million dollars for the month, or I will pay you one penny the first day, double that penny the next day, then double it again, and so on for a month. Well, if you said you'd take the penny, you'd earn $5,368,709.12 for the month! A very small thing can multiply very fast.

National Rally, 1991

Covering Home

I love baseball, and have all my life. I guess my favorite baseball player of all time is Nolan Ryan. I admired his skill as a record-breaking pitcher for many, many years and I appreciated his standard of excellence both on and off the field. He is truly a role model.

For Mother's Day one year, my son Tommy gave me a copy of Ruth Ryan's book, *Covering Home*. In the forward, Nolan wrote this of his wife, Ruth: "Ruth has always been there for me, always backing me up, always covering home."

What about us as members of the Premier team? Are we backing each other up? Are we there for each other? Are we always covering home?

The Two Shovels Story

$\mathcal{I}$ have a necklace that Peggy Horner designed and gave me for my birthday. It has two shovels. Let me tell you the story of this necklace.

Many years ago, my friend Mary Crowley met a student from South Africa, who was attending Dallas Theological Seminary. He was short of money to pay his tuition, and Mary made sure he was able to finish his studies with no debt. The day came for the graduation ceremonies and the student gave Mary a gift to show his gratitude for her benevolence. His brother in South Africa was a silversmith and he had fashioned a unique necklace for Mary. It was a pair of small silver shovels on a chain. One shovel was very tiny and the other was larger. The student explained that a philanthropist was once asked, "How can you give away so much, and have so much left?" He answered, "I really don't know. I just shovel it out and God shovels it in—and He has a bigger shovel." Whenever I wear this necklace, I'm reminded that we give with small shovels while God gives with a BIG one.

One of Joan's Favorite Stories

The Hostess and Your Success

H elp her to have a great show;
   make her look good.

O vercome her fear of failure
   with your confidence.

S elect great jewelry for everyone
   at the show to model.

T ime—spend it coaching your
   Hostess and encouraging her.

E nthuse about her show and
   she will pass it on.

S ervice your Hostess as if she
   were a queen. She is!

S uccess will be the end result.

WHAT'S YOUR SERVICE RATING?

We all understand the value of service. We believe that superior service is necessary if we are to grow in a successful manner. We all know that personal service has become a rare commodity in the marketplace today. But what is the definition of service? Service is the ability to deliver what you promise!

As Jewelers and Designers, what is your service rating? You can be a real leader in this area of service. You must first understand that service quality is a key ingredient to your success. Know this and believe it in your heart. Don't compromise. Serve your fellow Jewelers by being faithful to Premier meetings. There aren't that many scheduled, but you will be an encouragement by your support and attendance. Seek out opportunities to help a new Jeweler. Remember how you first felt going into a room full of strangers? If you sponsor others into this business, make a personal commitment to them to work with them to reach their goals. Coach them, correct them, praise them, listen to them. Keep good communication with them.

I think one of the essential characteristics of leaders in a service business is their own personal integrity. They are truthful, fair, consistent, always honest, and as a result, they will earn the respect of others. That is so necessary if one desires to be a

Designer and a leader in Premier. One definition of a leader, you know, is someone who has followers. And if you don't earn others' trust and respect, there are no followers.

And what about dealing with problems? If you are dedicated to serving, you'll find a way to handle problems in a positive way. Let's look at a few of these issues.

❋ **LOW-ATTENDANCE SHOWS**: Are you able to turn a "no-show" Training Show into a positive thing for a new Jeweler? That is a wonderful way to serve her.

❋ **BACKORDERS**: These are always distressing. I ordered the cutest shoes out of Bloomingdale's catalog and I haven't received them yet. But, you know, they send me a postcard every couple of weeks to apologize and to say they are hopeful the supplier can deliver next month. The delivery hasn't come, but I no longer am irritated because they made an attempt to explain and to keep in touch. I felt that they really cared. Couldn't we do that, too? Perhaps a call once in a while to acknowledge their backorder, or just to keep in touch with our customers. Keep that personal touch. That's good service.

❋ **RECEIVING BROKEN JEWELRY**: What an opportunity for service! Be proud to remind customers (and new Jewelers) of our

Golden Guarantee. That's a real service. And do stay in touch until that customer is absolutely satisfied.

These are all practical examples of commitment to quality service, and this is what Premier stands for.

National Rally, 1991

Our Perfect Example

Do you take delight in serving each other? Do you put the interests of others first? In Premier, commitment to service is our bottom line. In Matthew 20:28, we read that the Lord Jesus "did not come to be served, but to serve, and to give His life as a ransom for many." Jesus came to serve and He is our ultimate Perfect Example.

PRINCESS SERVANT HEARTS

*E*ver since I was a little girl in Canada, I have been fascinated with Royalty. I followed all the weddings where the different royal families of Europe would join together and I loved to read of the little Princesses who were born with those royal bloodlines. Once in a great while there would enter a commoner—one not of the royal lineage. He or she became part of the royal family by marriage. No one entered the royal family except by marriage or birth.

Not so with our Premier Royal Court of Princesses. They are not born a Princess, nor do they become a Princess by marriage. They are a chosen few.

In nearly every business I know anything about, employees, distributors and sales personnel are rewarded only for their selling or recruiting, for how they perform. It has long been a dream of Andy's that Premier's highest honor would be given not based on performance, but related to character and a serving heart. Andy's dream was wed with my love of royalty and the result was our Premier Princess Court.

A Premier Princess serves people and has an attitude of giving, encouraging, caring, sharing, and loving. She believes that Premier is a way of life and shows it in her own lifestyle.

I am very honored and privileged to be the Queen Mother to our Premier Royal Court of Princesses. They are a very special part of my life.

National Rally, approximately 1992

A Service Attitude

The starting point at Premier is "How may I serve you?" A servant attitude, more than any other trait, makes for a productive leader. It will take precedence over personality, skills, and education. Skills can be taught, education achieved, but a servant attitude is a matter of the heart and comes from the inner core of a person.

A servant will always be thinking, *What can I do for you?* Not, *What's in it for me?* The famous scientist Albert Schweitzer said, "The only ones among us who will really be happy are those who have sought and found how to serve."

PLEASE PASS THE BUTTER STORY

om Heinsohn, the explosive former Celtics basketball player and coach, was finishing lunch in a hotel coffee shop one day, when he called the waitress over and asked her for an extra pat of butter.

"I'm sorry," she said, "Only one butter pat per customer."

"Oh, come on," Heinsohn protested. "I can't eat the other half of my roll without any butter on it."

The waitress apologized, but politely explained again that the restaurant's policy called for only one pat of butter with each plate lunch. The rules were the same for everyone.

"Do you know who I am?" Heinsohn exploded.

"No," she said.

"I'm the coach of the Boston Celtics."

"Well, do you know who I am?" she shot back. Before Heinsohn could reply, the waitress scribbled out his check and put their relationship into proper perspective. "I'm the one who passes out the butter."

Now, just to keep our business in perspective, let's think a minute about who "passes out the butter" in Premier. Is it Andy and I? No. Is it the Home Office management team? No. Is it our Executive Directors and senior leadership in the field? No. The butter in Premier is passed out by our customers and our Hostesses. Best not to forget that.

One of Joan's Favorite Stories

Be a Giver

It's the givers in life that make the difference. These are the individuals who give of themselves without asking for or expecting anything in return. We must always remember that the source of giving is love; and the source of love is Jesus Christ.

G enerous with time and talent

I nspires others

V alues the success of others

E nthusiastic about life

R ecognizes the potential in others

S ervant's heart towards others

YOU ARE PREMIER'S FUTURE

The key to the future of Premier Designs is you! You have great influence with what you say and how you say it. The future of our company depends on the new leadership that you bring in and develop—the Premier way.

2009 Regional Rally

There was a king in the Old Testament named Josiah. He became king of Israel when he was eight years old, and he reigned for 31 years. This is how he was described, "He did what was right in the eyes of the Lord and followed completely the ways of his father David, not turning aside to the right or to the left" (2 Kings 22:2). Josiah did what was pleasing in the Lord's sight. He followed the example of his ancestor David. How would you like to have that said about you? That you did what was pleasing in the Lord's sight. That you followed the example of your upline. That you followed the Premier way!

We have been in business now well into our 24th year. Our growth has been steady and pretty incredible. Nearly every year we break some kind of record or another. God has been so good. But I want to remind you to "Give thanks to the Lord and proclaim His greatness, let the whole world know what He has done" (Psalm 105:1). That was our 2001 Verse of the Year.

As the Israelites were about to enter the Promised Land, Moses urged them never to forget how they had arrived at the new land and who had provided it for them. Over and over Moses reminded them that the land was a gift from God. Don't forget! Remember what God has done and remember your commitment.

I read this quote somewhere—I have no idea who said it, but I liked it and wrote it down. "Leadership without personal commitment to an unchanging standard leads to moral corruption, unethical behavior and erosion." It's not the standards that change, it's our actions. We see that all around us, even in high places of government. So, we need to commit to remember. We are reminded what God has done every year at our Rally when Andy does his session, "Lest We Forget."

Premier is God's company. It's not ours, it's not the CEO's or the President's. It's not the Executive Directors' company. If it were, we would surely fail! As leaders, remember your commitment to uphold the Philosophy, Purpose and Principles of Premier. Talk about these every time you are with your Premier children, day and night. We are very forgetful people and we all need constant reminders—to remember!

I once read this story in a church bulletin. In his classic novel, *One Hundred Years of Solitude*, Gabriel Garcia Marquez tells the story of a little village which is afflicted by a strange plague of forgetfulness—a kind of contagious amnesia. The plague went through the population rather quickly and caused people to forget the name of even the most common objects. One young man, still unaffected, tried to limit the damage by putting labels on everything. "This is a table, a window, a dog. This is a cow—it has to be milked every morning." At the entrance of the town, he put two large signs. One read, "The name of our village is Macondo." The larger of the two signs read, "God exists!"

Yes, God exists! He has raised Premier up for all of us. Let's not ever forget that. We can tell the Premier story over and over again to new Jewelers. They must be taught and reminded. You are Premier's future. We are counting on you to preserve this company that God has raised up—not for the glory of any human being, but for God's glory.

National Rally, 2009

JOAN, OUR QUEEN MOTHER

"I will bless the Lord at all times; His praise will continually be on my lips. Glorify the Lord with me; let us exalt His name together."

PSALM 34:1, 3

JOAN HORNER, OUR QUEEN MOTHER

*I*n a keepsake she prepared for her children, grandchildren and great-grandchildren a few years ago, Joan wrote, "I could fill volumes about what God has done in my life; the tapestry He was weaving, the picture He was painting, the purpose and mission He gave to me, and the difficulties His grace helped me to over-come—much of which I did not see or understand at the time, yet now I see clearly. It was all part of God's plan, all under His direc-tion. Remembering my stories has filled me with gratitude to the Lord for what He has done in me and through me."

JOAN'S EARLY YEARS

She was born Joan Vivian Taylor on May 12, 1925, in Woodstock, Ontario, Canada, to Elizabeth and Lionel Edward Linley Taylor. A few years later her brother, Ted, was born.

age 5 with mother and brother Ted

6 months old

Young Joan was a good student who loved to read. She excelled at writing and spelling, Latin and French. During these years Joan's life-long passion for baseball began to grow. Just how much Joan loved baseball is best exemplified by the fact that she quit two jobs because her bosses would not allow her to bring a radio to work and listen to the World Series. "I love my baseball!" she declared.

age 12

Throughout her life in Woodstock, Joan had many friends—she definitely had the gift of friendship and she cultivated it her entire life. She graduated from high school in 1941, at the age of 16, and enrolled in Woodstock Business College. She also joined the Canadian Red Cross Corps.

high school

HER SENTIMENTAL JOURNEY WITH ANDY

Joan first met Andy at elementary school in Woodstock; during high school they were friends. Of those days, Andy says, "I was actually courting Joan, even though she didn't know it."

Joan and Andy as teenagers

In 1945, back home on a 30-day leave from combat duty with the Royal Canadian Navy, Andy finally won Joan over during a series of nightly dates. Says Andy, "We never should have been together. I was a poor kid from the wrong side of the tracks and she was from a well-to-do family on the other side of town."

October, 1945

Joan and Andy married March 9, 1946, and immigrated to the United States in 1950, fulfilling Joan's life-long dream. It was in Dallas in 1951 that Joan turned her life over to Jesus Christ at the First Baptist Church. It was there that she met Mary Crowley, who immediately became her spiritual mentor and friend. Joan grew steadily in her faith and later took on many different teaching and leadership roles within the church.

March 9, 1946

From 1948 to 1975 Joan was a stay-at-home-mom raising five children—Andrea, Sarah, Tim, Mary and Tommy. Andy's jobs took them to Racine, Wisconsin, and Gladewater,

Andy & Joan outside their first apartment

Texas, before they finally settled for good in Dallas in 1964.

JOAN'S CAREER YEARS

In 1975, when their youngest son, Tommy, was in high school, Joan began traveling with Andy in his work with Home Interiors and Gifts field managers. He had been an executive with Home Interiors since 1967. Joan joined Home Interiors full-time in 1976, where she eventually served as traveling companion to long-time friend, mentor and Home Interiors' founder, Mary Crowley.

Mary, Jim, Tommy, Andrea & Sarah

Joan & Mary Crowley

Andy and Joan left Home Interiors in 1982, and in 1985, after much prayer and soul-searching, co-founded Premier Designs with the purpose of honoring God and serving people, enriching every life they could touch in the process.

In Joan's 25 years as executive vice president of Premier Designs, she oversaw design and selection of the extensive jewelry line. She also served as President of the Horner-Premier Foundation, which currently supports

Houston Rally, 1991

ministries, missions and charities in the U.S. and 62 other countries around the world.

National Rally, 2003

Joan was a soft-spoken encourager and mentor for Premier's Jewelers, legendary for her handwritten notes to offer support, and thanks and prayer. Joan's quiet grace, dignity and integrity in every circumstance made her the perfect "Queen Mother."

Under Joan and Andy's leadership, Premier Designs became highly successful and nationally recognized, despite the fact

Celebrating 25 years of service at National Rally, 2010

they insisted on conducting business in a way contrary to all popular corporate wisdom—by putting people first, before profits. Some of Joan and Andy's recent business accolades include:

- Ernst & Young Entrepreneurs of the Year, 2004
- Russell H. Perry Free Enterprise Award, 2007
- Direct Selling Association Hall of Fame, 2009
- Honorary Doctorates of Humanities, Dallas Baptist University, 2010

Above any of the honors accorded her by the world, however, Joan cherished her roles as wife, mother, and Christian. It's the fruits of those labors that are most often reflected in her spoken and written words that were referenced for this book.

The Horner Extended Family in 2008

Seated on floor–Ryan Figert, Justin Horner, Jessica Horner, Gaby Blois. Seated on sofas–Thomas & Caroline Horner; McKenzie Horner; Kathryn Horner; Drew Horner; Gavin, Alex & Erin Figert; Tommy, Donna & Jolie Horner; Caris & Juliannah Wetzel. Standing–Craig Callison; Peggy & Tim Horner; Grant Callison; Andrea Horner, Eric Billigmeier; Joan & Andy; Alex Morris & Ash Collins; Jack & Mary Collins; Sarah & Jake Wetzel; Miah & Dwain Confer